Praise for *ROAR!*

"What do you care about? Your company? A cause or campaign? Something you created? Is it as successful as it deserves to be? If so, good for you. If not, you need *Roar!* This page-turning book shows how to capture and keep the attention (and wallet) of your target customers so your priority projects get noticed and funded . . . for all the right reasons. Read it and reap."

—Sam Horn
Author of *POP! Stand Out in Any Crowd* and *Tongue Fu*

"*ROAR!* offers timeless marketing wisdom in a timely and entertaining package. Highly recommended."

—Michael J. Gelb
Author, *How to Think Like Leonardo da Vinci*

"*ROAR!* is a remarkable book, chock full of timeless wisdom and a must-read for anyone who has anything to do with sales or marketing. I've read just about every book on the topic that has been published over the past 10 years, and this one is the best by far. Get it!"

—Peter Economy
Associate Editor, *Leader to Leader* magazine
Author, *Managing for Dummies*

"*ROAR!* provides a simple memorable process that will help our franchisees understand and win over prospects. It's a worthy addition to any customer experience training process."

—Brian Scudamore
Founder and CEO, 1-800-GOT-JUNK?

"*ROAR!* is a highly clever and entertaining read. *ROAR!* is a great way to understand the importance of creating value for the customer, and I would recommend this book to any entrepreneur—or entrepreneur-to-be."

—Kathleen Allen, PhD
Director, USC Marshall Center
for Technology Commercialization
Professor, USC Lloyd Greif Center
for Entrepreneurial Studies

"Kevin Daum and Dan Turner have written the book that cuts through the multitude of sales and marketing messages that now overwhelm your prospective customers. The power of *ROAR!* works. It's time to get it working for you and your business."

—Robert "Jake" Jacobs
CEO, Winds of Change Group
Author, *Real Time Strategic Change* &
You Don't Have to Do It Alone

"I loved *ROAR!* Its lessons are written in a compelling story that anyone can relate to and learn from. The ROAR system is a simple way to help our students impress other people with their value in the real world, and we will now look to see how we can make ROAR part of our curriculum."

—Gary Tuerack
President and Founder, The National Society of
Leadership and Success

"Kevin Daum has taken the sales process to a whole new level of simplicity. I wish I had this information 20 years ago; it might have made the 10 companies I have owned a little easier to grow and develop."

—Troy Hazard
Author, *The Naked Entrepreneur*
Former Chairman, The Entrepreneur's Organization

"Sales and marketing continues to be an overlooked part of every successful business story in American history. Kevin Daum focuses his spotlight on this often-overlooked part of every successful business story, and he honors history by letting us learn new insights from a wise business teacher."

—Dr. Blaine McCormick
Author, *Ben Franklin: America's Original Entrepreneur*
Associate Professor of Management,
Baylor University, Hankamer School of Business

"A great story, especially the compelling value proposition development. I would recommend it for any company we're working with. And—it's a great airplane read."

—Gary Moon
Managing Director, Ridgecrest Capital Partners

"A fun, easy to read, and brilliant business book. I've passed along copies of *ROAR!* for our management team and we've already begun implementing the ROAR concept."

—Dennis Hoffman
President, CashBox

"*ROAR!* is that rare find in business texts—fundamental truth presented in actionable format; I am recommending it to every entrepreneur I know."
—Kathy Odell
Director, Pacific Capital Bancorp

"In *ROAR!* Kevin Daum has captured a very important dimension of the buyer's psyche that sellers must consider if they want to capture more deals."
—Howard Shore
Principal, Activate Group, Inc.

"Not only was *ROAR!* fun and informative for my company, I am passing on the concepts to my clients to help them communicate in a compelling manner as well."
—Barry Cohn
Managing Partner, Cohn Handler & Co.,
Certified Public Accountant

"As a senior sales leader at an innovative and nimble software company, I found *ROAR!* to be an excellent parable for my sales team. Not only could they sink their teeth into the impeccably described meals, they could also learn from the book."
—Jeff Benjamin
Vice President of Sales, Ellie Mae

"Kevin's latest book can be your new V.P.: It has a Very Pertinent Valuable Premise, sure to make you Victorious and Profitable, and ready to help you take advantage of your Vast Potential!"
—Paul Levitan
President and CEO, Galaxy Desserts

"Finally in *ROAR!* I found a book that is both inspiring and practical. Mr. Daum has a keen grasp of how to understand customers, and his work was an inspiration to our team as we seek to make our message more effective and more relevant."

—Justin Paul Hersh
President and CEO, Group Delphi

"I love the simple effectiveness of *ROAR!* My team has completely integrated the four buyer concept into every aspect of our customer communication protocols. Kevin Daum's approach fully delivers an easy method to teach your sales team valuable tools in a sticky, entertaining way."

—Christina Harbridge
Mischief Executive Officer, Allegory, Inc.

"Daum simplifies a 3,500-year-old model and makes it relevant to today's challenging economy. *ROAR!* will tell you how to integrate sales and marketing and turn your business into a roaring success."

—Les Rubenovitch
President, Winning Edge Consultants Inc.

"I highly recommend this clever and amusing kosher culinary journey of New York, painlessly delivering a memorable marketing and sales strategy. *ROAR!* is an important and accessible resource for any executive."

—Phyllis Caskey
President and CEO,
Hollywood Entertainment Museum

"*ROAR!* is simply brilliant! The story is engaging and the message is powerful and clear. If *ROAR!* doesn't make your sales roar, I don't know what will."

—Mo Fathelbob
President, Forum Resources Network
Author, *Forum: The Secret Advantage of Successful Leaders*
Former Executive Director, Entrepreneurs' Organization

"I was extremely impressed by the message and enjoyable delivery in *Roar!* I do believe the book far exceeds the 'Oh yea, I knew that' which is the common reaction when one reads these types of things. I love the freshness in this approach to sales. I believe in its value enough that I am sending it to many of my CEO clients."

—Timothy R. Chrisman
Chairman of the Federal Home Loan Bank of San Francisco

"Roar! offers timeless marketing wisdom in a timely and entertaining package. Highly recommended."

—Michael J. Gelb
Author of *How to Think Like Leonardo Da Vinci*

ROAR!

GET HEARD IN THE SALES AND MARKETING JUNGLE

A BUSINESS FABLE

KEVIN DAUM
WITH DANIEL A. TURNER

WILEY

John Wiley & Sons, Inc.

Published by John Wiley & Sons, Inc., Hoboken, New Jersey.
Published simultaneously in Canada.

For general information on our other products and services or for technical support, please contact our Customer Care Department within the United States at (800) 762-2974, outside the United States at (317) 572-3993 or fax (317) 572-4002.

Wiley also publishes its books in a variety of electronic formats. Some content that appears in print may not be available in electronic books. For more information about Wiley products, visit our web site at www.wiley.com.

ISBN: 978-0470-59879-5

Printed in the United States of America.

10 9 8 7 6 5 4 3 2 1

For Kevin's Forum and wee Miriam

"Words are, of course, the most powerful drug used by mankind."

—RUDYARD KIPLING

Contents

Chapter 1

The Meeting

RYAN MILLER was 22 years into his career in sales and marketing and he'd hit a wall. He was the Vice President of Sales and Marketing for Wolfson Furnishings, a well-established furniture company. An employee-owned company, Wolfson sold office furniture and systems through retail outlets and through its web site. Ryan had led the charge to establish an online presence, and the site was now directly or indirectly involved in more than half of all new sales. For the majority of the time Ryan had been at Wolfson, things had been pretty good. Wolfson had focused on law firms and software companies, and because they were both growing quickly in the 1980s and 1990s, they had seen no need to branch out into additional industries. Their chosen client base had money to spend and there was lots of business to go around all the companies that focused on them. Ryan had been well paid, with stock and stock options, and had figured he had it made.

But now things were difficult. Lately, Wolfson had been struggling. The economy was rough. Businesses were closing—both clients' and competitors'. With massive layoffs throughout the industry, the long-term relationships Wolfson had been cultivating were gone. Everybody had cut back, and the marketing materials Ryan's people were using were having little effect in getting appointments. Even when his salespeople could get appointments, they couldn't close the deal.

Ryan was concerned for the company. He was also concerned about morale. If business slowed any more, the company would have to lay off more people, and they had already reduced staff twice; they were now down by 50 percent from the prior year.

But Ryan was even more concerned for his family. With two boys in high school and college expenses starting the following year, he had been counting on his stock to get them through that comfortably—and his ownership shares were becoming worthless. His wife Christina earned decent money at her job as an underwriter with a boutique insurance company, but certainly not enough to support their home and lifestyle in Short Hills, a well-to-do suburb in New Jersey. If Ryan couldn't get sales and marketing back on track, Wolfson would be on the road to bankruptcy and he would be looking for a job in an environment that was anything but friendly. And Christina's job wasn't looking all that stable, either, given the big changes in the insurance industry and layoffs rampant in her company.

Sitting at Penn Station, sweating from the summer heat and waiting for his train home, Ryan fantasized about trading it all in and joining the Peace Corps. His reverie was interrupted when he heard someone behind him call out, "Ryan? Is that you my old friend?"

Ryan turned around and saw a portly Hasidic man with a big smile on his face. Ryan had seen Hasidic Jews before. New York was a center of Hasidic life, so they were a common sight in most parts of the city and in many nearby suburbs. Ryan was accustomed to their long black coats, long hair and beards, and of course their trademark broad-brimmed black fedoras. He had often wondered how they could stand to wear all that heavy black clothing in this summer humidity. But Ryan couldn't remember knowing any Hasidic Jews personally. Ryan had gone to Livingston High School (sole claim to fame: matriculated Jason Alexander), which had had a substantial Jewish population, so he certainly knew a lot of Jews. But as a nonreligious Christian himself, he had not interacted with anyone with a serious religious identity in many years.

"Do I know you?" Ryan asked, confused.

"Do you know me?" The stranger asked with a hint of sarcasm attached. "We know each other ten years, go to high school, I even let you date my sister! I mean, sure, she dumped you, but did that affect your memory? Or did you get a knock on the keppe at that fancy college?"

Ryan couldn't believe his ears. "Lenny? Is that really you?!" After high school, Ryan headed down to Georgetown University in Washington, and he hadn't seen Lenny since. He was shocked that Lenny recognized him 26 years later, and even more shocked at the change in Lenny.

Lenny had been a skinny kid with a buzz cut and an attitude. Now he was big, a lion of a man, with a massive beard covering much of his face and curly sideburns cascading down out of his black hat. Ryan remembered Lenny's family being religious. They were kosher, if he remembered correctly, but this was ridiculous. "Lenny, when did you become, you know, all this?" he asked, indicating the hat, clothing, and hair.

Lenny laughed. "Yeah, I guess you didn't get the memo. While you were living it up in DC I spent five glorious years at Rutgers University, just an hour from home, though I lived on campus instead of commuting. So while I was there I started going to a religious center called Chabad house, which had the best kosher food on campus. I didn't grow up around many really observant people, and the devotion of the people in Chabad really appealed to me. They spent so much time studying the Torah!" Ryan remembered that the Torah was the Jews' name for their Bible and other religious tracts. Lenny continued, happy to tell a story he had clearly told many times before. "The Torah scholars I met on trips to New York always impressed me, too. I'd always wanted to spend more time studying Torah, so a few years back I figured, why not go all the way?"

Lenny explained that after college he had built a good packaging business. "I was blessed with success and leisure time," he said. "I got married, had two daughters and a son, became a family man. Here, take a look." Lenny pulled out his iPhone and showed Ryan pictures of his family.

"Lovely," Ryan commented. "I have a couple of kids myself." Ryan pulled up the picture of his family on his BlackBerry. "Teenagers," he said, shrugging off any reasonable explanation of the goth-looking boys staring out at them.

Lenny laughed. "Ah, well, family life is a blessing in itself."

"I guess. But I'm confused," Ryan said, changing the subject. "Did you sell your packaging business? Is that why you have the time to study?"

"No, no, no, of course not," replied Lenny. "But we have great people and great systems, so I don't need to spend a lot of time running it. We make lots of sales, we deliver lots of product, and life is good, kineahora!"

"Your sales are still good? Even in this economy?" Ryan asked skeptically.

"Actually, we're doing even better now than we did last year."

Ryan was perplexed. Everyone he knew was having trouble. He had some knowledge of Lenny's sector—one of his friends used to be in the packaging business before his company went under last year; it was just as tough there as everywhere else. How could Lenny's company be growing in sales with everyone struggling around him?

Ryan let his skepticism show: "Come on, Lenny. I run sales and marketing for a fifty-year-old furnishing company, and man, it's been rough lately. How is it, with the slowing economy, that you are doing so well? Is your packaging that good? Is it so different from all the other stuff out there?"

Lenny chuckled. "Well, I like to think our product is pretty good, but no, I wouldn't say it's groundbreaking, if that's what you mean. To tell you the truth, I actually chalk it up to our sales and marketing approach. I think that's what's kept us going and growing all these years, through both good and bad economic times."

Now Lenny had Ryan's full attention. "Really!" Ryan said. "What are you doing that's so special and new?"

"I'm not sure I would call it special," said Lenny, "and it's definitely not new. In fact it's a pretty straightforward method that's been used for roughly 3,500 years."

Ryan was sure his high school friend was pulling his leg. The only working sales process that had been around that long was "sex sells," and packaging was one of the least sexy products Ryan could imagine. "I suppose next you'll tell me that Socrates invented CRM."

Lenny chuckled and started to answer, then caught the schedule board out of the corner of his eye. "Listen, Ryan," Lenny said. "I have to catch my train. Why don't you meet me for lunch at my office on Monday and I'll show you what we've been doing? Give me your card; here's mine. Come around eleven and we'll catch up over a nice steak. I know a great place."

Ryan glanced at Lenny's card and promised to be there. After all, he figured, the way things were going, what did he have to lose?

As he settled in on the train home he looked at Lenny's card:

Golden Box Packaging

Lenny Goldstein
Founder and CEO

718-555-1000   4248 18th Avenue
len@nonakedproduct.com   Brooklyn, NY 11218

On the back was a URL—www.NoNakedProduct.com.

Ryan smiled and thought, "Hmm, original URL. Geez, you wouldn't think a guy steeped in religious studies would be going around talking about nakedness. And then he got it: packaging was like covering the nakedness of a product. He smiled, both at the cleverness of the line and at his own thickheadedness in missing the meaning the first time. It must be the heat—and the fact that Wolfson's business problems were getting him down.

He got on his train thinking about Lenny's sister Miriam. She was his first girlfriend. They'd had some great times . . . until she dropped him to date that jock when he'd left for college. Ouch!

Chapter 2

Visiting the V.P.

MONDAY JUST BEFORE 11 o'clock, Ryan marveled at the Brooklyn neighborhood in which Lenny had chosen to grow Golden Box Packaging, Inc. It seemed to be a mixture of business and residential buildings, and most of the men were wearing hats like Lenny's or the black skull-caps. The area was busy but not wealthy; the cars parked on the streets were almost entirely functional—SUVs, caravans, old clunkers. The cars parked outside Lenny's building were nicer, but still modest. The building itself was almost indistinguishable from the ones near it, red brick and stone, with a sign bearing the Golden Box logo. Inside, Ryan was relieved to be in the air-conditioning, out of the late August heat. The company was obviously doing well. There was a buzz in the place that signaled a positive, growing business.

While he waited (Lenny was finishing a call, the recep-tionist told Ryan), he picked up a Golden Box brochure from the coffee table and noticed that the design and language was very similar to the web site he had visited over the weekend. He smiled again at the cleverness of the Web URL, www.NoNakedProduct.com, and liked the way Lenny's marketing people had tied the copy to that theme. He also noticed one of the pizza boxes that had been highlighted on the web site. Apparently many pizza restaurants didn't recognize the beautiful canvas they had available for marketing messages. Lenny's company had helped increase revenues at several pizza places by "clothing" their pizza boxes with advertisements for pizza and even for other products. Ryan mused that he'd probably buy more pizza if his favorite place had similar coupons on their boxes for other local services.

Just then Lenny walked out and greeted Ryan warmly. "Come into my office. We'll chat for a bit and then we can head off to lunch."

They wound their way through several large rooms of busy people working at their desks, talking on the phone, and talking with one another in low tones. "You've built quite a company here," Ryan said.

"We're pretty happy," Lenny responded. "We have about 120 people working here, and they do a great job. We're a sales-driven company, and we've found a sales process that works well for us."

"You mean this 3,500-year process?" Ryan asked skeptically.

Lenny smiled, "Yes, that." He paused and looked thoughtful. "But before I am ready to share that process with you, I should really introduce you to our V.P. of sales and marketing."

"Great!" exclaimed Ryan, "I would love to meet him!"

Lenny grinned knowingly. "Did you visit our web site?"

"Of course, it's always the first thing I do whenever I get a business card or meet someone."

"I figured you might," Lenny said. "Most people do these days. I do it myself."

"So you've been to ours as well, then?" Ryan asked gingerly. The web site was his responsibility, and although it had been moderately effective in generating some online leads and home office sales, it wasn't bringing in the customers or orders it once did.

"Yes, and quite honestly that's the reason I think I should introduce you to our V.P. before we talk about our 3,500-year-old process. One won't do you much good without the other. The good news is that since you've been to the Golden Box web site, you've already seen the V.P. of sales and marketing."

As they arrived at a hallway that obviously housed the company's executives, Ryan thought for a second. He had gone through the site thoroughly. He remembered the listings of the management team, but didn't remember seeing a "Vice President of sales and marketing." There was an operations VP and a business development VP, but he would have remembered the sales and marketing person since he held the same title for his company.

They arrived in Lenny's office. "Here you are. This is our V.P.," beamed Lenny, as he pointed to a large plaque on the wall. The plaque read:

Golden Box Value Proposition

The Pain We Solve

Some products shouldn't be sold naked. Most food, electronic and other consumer products need packaging for storage, protection and preservation.

But packaging adds cost.

The Best Solution

Products should be clothed attractively in a cost-effective, creative manner that compels the buyer to purchase more products.

Why We Are the Best Solution Provider

We employ creative experts to help make your good ideas great.

Our small-run capability gives us flexibility.

Our volume gives us the best resources at discount prices.

www.NoNakedProduct.com

Ryan stared at the plaque for a moment. "Ah," he said. "Right, cute play on words. V.P., value proposition." Of course Ryan was familiar with the term. He had helped develop the value proposition for Wolfson Furnishings. It was a list of 10 features that, Wolfson executives believed, made the company better than their competition. It certainly wasn't as clean and concise as this, but this didn't seem to have nearly the depth of Wolfson's list. And it didn't talk about pain, which Ryan appreciated because he figured doing so was probably a downer.

Of course, looking at the plaque, it certainly seemed clear and compelling. He abruptly realized that the value proposition, the web site, and the marketing materials all played on the naked versus clothed concept. It was creative and certainly distinguished Golden Box from other companies. "Huh! How'd you develop this?"

"Before I answer that, there's one more thing I want to show you, then I'll explain over lunch. Let me grab my hat." Lenny grabbed his fedora and placed it on top of the yarmulke he was already wearing. "Oh, and here's a copy of our V.P. We give it out to all our people, and I think you'll find it helpful for our conversation." Lenny pressed a small laminated copy of the V.P. into Ryan's hand. As they started the walk back through the large rooms with the desks, Lenny whispered to Ryan, "OK. Pick any of my people and pretend to be a customer." Interested, Ryan nodded toward a young attractive brunette just hanging up the phone. Ryan noticed on her desk she had a copy of the V.P. attached with a clip to a little figurine of a lion. He looked around and realized that every desk had the same little lion figurine with a clip holding the card.

"Good choice," smiled Lenny. "Courtney, please come over here for a moment. I would like you to meet a long-time friend of mine, Ryan. Ryan, this is Courtney Franks. Courtney is one our most successful salespeople. Courtney, we're headed out for lunch, but before we go Ryan has a question for you."

Courtney smiled and shook the hand Ryan extended. "What can I help you with, Ryan?" Courtney asked.

"Could you briefly explain to me why I would want to do business with Golden Box? I mean, why you instead of one of your competitors?" Ryan inquired.

"I would be happy to," said Courtney. "I assume you're evaluating our company because you have something that requires packaging." Ryan nodded. "Good. Well, we don't want your product sitting out there on the shelf naked, do we?"

Ryan couldn't help but smile. Courtney continued. "I also assume you have concerns about how the packaging is going to add additional cost to your product. We've found that the best way to solve this problem is to create attractive packaging with a sales message that sells more of your product. That way you can recoup some of your packaging cost from the messaging.

"At Golden Box we have some distinct advantages over our competition to help you build such a solution. First, unlike our competitors we keep creative packaging experts on staff so we can work with your marketing people to create effective messaging in attractive packaging." She winked at Ryan and subtly smoothed her shirt against her side. "*Clothing,* as we like to call it." Ryan laughed.

"Second, while we can do large runs, we have the ability to do small runs as well, so we can test different packaging options and quickly change to the option that works best.

"Finally, and I hope this addresses your biggest concern, we do a lot of work with major suppliers. Our large volume gets us great discounts on materials, allowing us to pass that savings back to you."

Courtney stopped. There it was, as efficient and compelling as the plaque itself. The whole conversation took less than a minute and she had clearly communicated the entire value proposition in a clear and attractive manner. She had identified key differentiations between Golden Box and their competition. And all in less than the time it would take an elevator to get from lobby to penthouse for a cocktail party.

"Thank you, Courtney," Ryan said. "That was extremely helpful."

"Happy to oblige," Courtney replied. "Let me know if I can help with anything else. Enjoy your lunch." Courtney returned to her desk.

Ryan turned back to Lenny, thinking hard. Courtney was obviously a smart woman. No wonder she was a top salesperson. He really liked the way she kept to the script, but also seemed to make it her own. Of course, this was the luck of the draw. He'd obviously happened to pick a rainmaker.

Lenny sensed Ryan's skepticism. "Pick another." Ryan looked around and pointed at a young guy sitting in the middle of the office a good distance from Courtney's desk.

Lenny called out, "Gary, could you come over here for a moment?" Again Lenny whispered an aside to Ryan, "Gary has been with us in sales for about four months. He's doing fairly well for a newbie. Fresh out of Rutgers, still a frat boy." Ryan knew how hard it was to get these newly minted college kids to follow the company line. They all seemed to either want to do it their own way to prove something to the boss, or they wanted all the reward with none of the work.

Gary was introduced and the inquiry began. Although Gary didn't personalize the Value Proposition as well as Courtney did, he still did a very effective job of communicating each point without his delivery sounding canned or disingenuous. Ryan thanked Gary for his time and turned to Lenny.

"Would you like to try one more?" asked Lenny.

"No, I have a feeling they will all do just as well. Very impressive. You must have an intense sales training program."

"It's good enough," shrugged Lenny, "but truth be told, it didn't do us much good until we got the messaging right. We struggled for a long time with getting our people to say the same things, let alone the right things. Not because what they were saying wasn't true, but mostly because what we had them saying wasn't compelling or memorable. It wasn't until we nailed our Value Proposition that everyone started to really become aligned with our sales process."

Lenny led Ryan out the door. "Come on, I'm starved. Let's talk over lunch, and I'll explain why it works so well."

A short walk later, Lenny guided Ryan into a kosher Argentinean restaurant, El Gaucho Glatt. Ryan was slightly aware of the post-WWII connection between Jews and South America, but just like in the old days, Lenny never ceased to surprise him. The smell of meat wafted over them, and Ryan felt a little relieved they were going to a meat restaurant. He didn't mind eating in kosher restaurants that were either meat or dairy (which couldn't be mixed), but he really wasn't much for vegetarian food. Of course, he knew his odds of getting a Reuben sandwich or a BLT were definitely nil. Being kosher was really limiting—he couldn't imagine restricting his food like that!

They were guided to one of the tables near the kitchen and were soon eating a fantastic appetizer of marinated beef tongue, which Ryan couldn't recall having tried since he'd dined with Lenny's family one Sabbath evening in high school. He was positive it hadn't been this good in high school.

A good salesman, Ryan made sure he had his notepad and pen out so he could jot down a reminder to himself when he heard something useful. As they finished their appetizers and waited for their steaks, Ryan started asking questions.

"So this V.P. of sales and marketing, this is the key to your success in this market?" Ryan asked.

"It's part of it. It was a necessary step before we could apply the . . ."

"I know, I know!" Ryan interrupted impatiently. "The supersecret 3,500-year process."

"Don't worry, my friend," Lenny said. "We'll get to it. But the V.P. is key; otherwise, you'll never get to use the 3,500-year-old process."

"All right, fine," Ryan retorted as their steaks arrived. "Go for it. Tell me how this V.P. came about."

Over a really great steak—perfectly cooked and juicy—Lenny explained that he had attended a conference on raising venture capital back in the 1990s, when dot-coms were just entering the mainstream. Most of the conference was useless, but there was this one speaker who talked about pitching venture capitalists and used this model of *pain, solution,* and *best provider.*

Lenny told Ryan how the notes had sat in a drawer collecting dust until a few months after the dot-coms were no more, when sales were sluggish and he had been frustrated with lackluster performance from his sales crew. He had hired and fired more sales managers than he could remember and, exasperated, had gone to his notes looking for anything that would turn the business around. That's when he reacquainted himself with this Value Proposition concept. He brought in Courtney and a couple of other producing salespeople and together over time they identified the three components. The Golden Box V.P. of sales and marketing was born.

"So why does this Value Proposition work so well?" Ryan asked.

"Well, first there's the mechanics of the V.P.," explained Lenny. "Many value propositions at other companies are either one sentence or a laundry list of features that only take into account what executives think makes their company better than the competition. They assume the potential customer already knows why they're approaching the company."

"I'm not sure I follow," said Ryan. "Isn't a value proposition supposed to tout what your company does best? And why would a customer come to your company if he didn't need you?"

"Well, sure, the V.P. should talk to your company's best qualities," replied Lenny, "but what good is pushing your solution if you and your customer don't understand or agree on the problem in the first place? In today's market there's a lot of messaging out there, and answers become much more compelling when the customer identifies with the questions."

"Hmm, valid point. All right, tell me about the first statement in your V.P. I don't know if I like this *pain* idea." Ryan grimaced. "It sounds so negative."

Lenny nodded. "Yeah, I felt that way myself, at first. But then I understood. We're not creating pain for people. The pain is already there. Their products really are naked, and clothing them really does have costs. We're looking to articulate it clearly so that the customers who already feel that pain can find us."

Ryan was intrigued. He'd often had problems getting his salespeople to show customers that Wolfson cared about them, rather than about the salesperson's own commissions.

Lenny continued. "We immediately demonstrate that we understand the pain customers are already feeling.

This helps them progress down the sales process. When they hear us state the pain, and they identify with it, our credibility level is immediately raised in their minds. By providing this statement, we're doing something that's unfortunately considered very rare in business." Ryan looked quizzical, and Lenny chuckled. "We're showing empathy."

"Huh!" Ryan grunted.

"Once the pain is established, we provide resolution to the pain with an objective solution. In our case we say that products should be clothed such that the buyer wants to buy more product."

"Yeah, I noticed that," Ryan said. "Why is it objective? Why not just hit them with your features right there and then?"

Lenny leaned forward, excited, as he got to the good stuff. "People don't like to be sold. By giving them an objective solution to the pain, they are still absorbing and identifying information in an open manner. If we hit them with the features now, they'll put their guard back up and may get defensive."

"Fascinating," Ryan thought. "These guys have really thought this through."

"Of course, the solution has to be exactly on target," Lenny continued. "It must be the most obvious answer to the pain. The really cool part is that when the solution is on point, it resonates perfectly with the pain and the customer gets a big *Aha!* That emotional impact with the customer makes us look like very smart experts. Now the customer is receptive to how well we know our business and their issues. At this point, much of the initial sales job is done."

Ryan thought for a moment, moving the remains of his steak around his plate, then asked, "Doesn't the pain and solution statement become limiting? What if a potential client isn't concerned about the cost on their packaging or doesn't want to advertise on the package . . . or doesn't really feel they need packaging at all?"

"Ah," Lenny nodded, pleased. "First of all, I'm not sure I know of anyone who feels they're paying too little for their packaging. But look, we're not out to convert the whole world to our way of thinking. We can't be everything to all customers. So this helps not only to attract like-minded customers, but also to repel those we'll probably never close. This creates much greater efficiency in our sales process. My salespeople don't have to spend a lot of time selling people who most likely will never buy. The salespeople are happier because their sales percentages are higher and they don't waste time on difficult sales."

"All right," said Ryan. His writing hand was starting to hurt—he was getting so much good stuff! He thought for a moment, then pulled out his copy of the Golden Box V.P. "So I love the way the 'Best Solution Provider' part works," Ryan commented. "How'd you get your pitch so clear and compelling on what makes Golden Box the best solution provider?"

"I have to admit, for this part I had help," Lenny confessed. "At first we struggled to make it concise. Like you, we had a long list of features, but, truthfully, not all of them were that interesting or different from our competition. Some didn't even really relate to the pain we were identifying. This was part of the reason our sales-people were struggling. They were all presenting differ-ent sets of features. They would talk about the features they thought were interesting or sometimes just the ones they remembered. Some of the statements were stuff our competitors were also claiming.

"Their pitches were clumsy, inconsistent, and mostly ineffective. Customers were walking away with different perspectives of what Golden Box was all about. It was very rarely compelling. We didn't even have agreement on which customers we were trying to sell to! Once we whittled down to three differentiating features that related to the pain we identified and the solution we pre-sented, it was easy for our salespeople to get their pitch down and start attracting clients."

"So what sort of help did you get?" Ryan asked.

"We brought in a business growth guru to work with us on creating what he calls a brand promise. He told us that the heart of our marketing message had to be a clear statement of the three reasons we truly matter to a customer and that also make us different from our competitors.

"We used his material, looked at what we were doing differently than our competitors, and used the criteria to form the last statement. It's worked well."

"Interesting. I'll look him up online," said Ryan. "Hmm. I think we may need to work on revamping our value proposition. Actually, I think we need to work on creating one in the first place. It seems like such a simple set of statements, though. Does a short pitch like that really make the sale for you?

"Generally, no," Lenny replied. "It's a conversation starter. It needs to be quick and memorable. But it should be rich enough to get the customer interested in moving forward. If they hear you say it, they should want to know more. If they see it in your collateral, they should want to go to your web site, and if they see it on your home page, they should want to click on specific phrases to dig in further on the site."

"Interesting."

"It's also a conversation ender if done correctly," Lenny continued. "If you present it to prospects and they don't relate to the empathy, then you know they aren't the right customers for you. That saves you time and resources."

"I like that," Ryan noted. "Is there anything else I need to know about the value proposition before we get started on rewriting it?"

Lenny paused to think for a moment. "The key is that the V.P. has to be pervasive. It must be the core of all of your marketing materials, including your web site. And make it true and meaningful so your salespeople don't feel conflicted when they go out to sell it. Your people have to make it their own and be consistent in the way they deliver it. If it's not memorable for your sales team, then it's probably not going to be memorable for your clients either."

Lenny started, and checked his watch. He tossed some twenties on the table and stood up. "Hey, Ryan, I've gotta go. I booked another meeting for after lunch, and I just barely have time to get back to the office."

"Wait! What about the 3,500-year-old secret?" Ryan asked.

"Describing the process the right way will take a long time, my friend. I'm happy to share it another time. Next week starts the High Holidays, then Sukkot, and then the fall trade shows. . . . I won't be around for at least six weeks. Tell you what," Lenny said. "You've got a lot to do if you're going to revamp your V.P. Call me when you have it figured out and we'll get together again. Hey, it was really great seeing you, Ryan!"

And with that Lenny left the restaurant.

As the check came (less than Lenny had dropped—apparently he had paid for Ryan's lunch), Ryan looked through the notes he had taken during their discussion. He knew his machine was nowhere near as well oiled as the sales division at Golden Box, and suddenly realized he had a lot of work to do.

"Fine," he thought. Before the CEO of Wolfson Furnishings has reason to fire the current VP of sales and marketing, Ryan would bring in a new V.P.—a new value proposition, that is.

Chapter 3

Following Up

IT WAS A BRISK FALL DAY. Lenny was walking in Brooklyn admiring the quickly changing colors of the leaves when his iPhone began to vibrate. He grabbed it and saw it was an e-mail from Ryan.

Lenny,
    Vp working great. C attached. Ready for 3,500-year process. Lmk when we can meet.
    Ryan

Lenny opened the attachment and read it. Pleased to see his friend's excellent progress, Lenny e-mailed Ryan.

Ryan,
    This looks great! Let's meet next Monday for lunch. My office, 11 A.M.
    Lenny

"Buzz buzz!" Apparently Ryan had responded.

Great! C u there!
    RM

Wolfson Furnishings Value Proposition

The Pain We Solve

Conveying a great image and preventing health problems is difficult when furniture is old and worn.

The Best Solution

New furniture that is ergonomic, attractive, and cost-effective can be installed to improve health and image issues.

Why We Are the Best Solution Provider

We have in-house ergonomic and design experts.

Our products are certified green and recyclable and can be traded in for credit.

We finance in-house for all credit scenarios with flexible terms.

www.WorkBetterLiveBetter.com

Chapter 4

The 3,500-Year-Old Process

RYAN was in a hurry to get to Brooklyn. He didn't want to be one minute late for his meeting with Lenny, and the Monday train to Manhattan from New Jersey had been delayed, messing up his schedule for the day. Lenny had sent him information for a restaurant in Flatbush, so Ryan bounded onto the Q train at Herald Square. As he found a seat, he reflected on the work he had done over the past few months. He had much to discuss with Lenny.

Lunch with Lenny had set in motion a lot of activity at Wolfson Furnishings on the value proposition. Figuring out their V.P. had not been an easy process. There was a lot of discussion, debate, and even a few heated arguments, but it had been worth it. Lenny hadn't given much direction on how to create the V.P., so Ryan had to develop his own process. He started by interviewing all his sales and marketing people to see what they were actually saying to customers. He compared his interview notes with the text used on the Wolfson web site and in the collateral and noted all the inconsistencies.

After compiling a complete list of the statements and phrases being used, Ryan involved the other vice presidents at Wolfson to get their feedback and buy-in into the process. Then he picked a small team representing sales, marketing, and management and held several meetings with a trusted outside facilitator whom they had used previously.

The facilitator was able to get everyone to participate in open discussion, helping narrow down the company's strategic focus so they could understand the real pain they were trying to solve. It took several sessions to come to an agreement, but once they nailed it the obvious solution was, well, obvious, so they moved on to differentiation.

Identifying Wolfson's differentiating factors took several more meetings. His people struggled with being objective about Wolfson's strengths relative to those of their competitors. Some got stuck, coming back over and over again to their claim of "excellent customer service." But Ryan was adamant that everyone in every business, including their competitors, claimed excellent customer service, even if they didn't provide it. Ryan understood that these differentiators needed to be something their competitors couldn't offer, at least not easily or without great expense. The facilitator was a big help in getting everyone to focus on what really made Wolfson different.

Ryan also found it was difficult to wordsmith the V.P. statements in the sessions, so he would often take away the notes and work with his favorite copywriter from marketing to tease out just the right phrases from the ideas in the sessions. He could then go back and share these with everyone for feedback and approval.

Finally, with the V.P. down pat, he'd presented it to the entire executive management team, including the CEO. After some minor wordsmithery, the CEO had fully bought into it and had worked with him to convince the CFO to approve the expenditures needed to revamp their web site and collateral materials to reflect the new approach. They'd made the changes to the web site but were still working on the rest of their collateral. Ryan figured they had a couple more months to go on that effort.

Already with just the changes they'd made to the web site and to sales training, Wolfson Furnishings was starting to see results. Since they'd put the new material on the web site, leads had increased nearly 10 percent month over month and over the same month the prior year, even given the less robust economy. Salespeople were starting to sound consistent and felt comfortable using the new V.P. The number of appointments had increased dramatically. Closing customers was now the biggest challenge, but at least they were getting more opportunities, and that was giving a boost to sales. He was even feeling happier at home, although his kids didn't help any. He'd been talking to Christina about the V.P. processes, and she was working to apply it to herself, thinking it'd help her with her work issues as well.

About a half-hour later the train stopped at the Avenue J station and Ryan dashed out and up the stairs. He headed west toward East 15th. He looked up from his BlackBerry after checking for e-mail and spotted the restaurant, Estihana. "Huh! Who knew they had kosher sushi?" Ryan thought, bemused.

Ryan walked in the door and saw Lenny seated at a table far in the corner. He walked over and Lenny stood up to greet Ryan warmly and shake his hand vigorously. "How are you, my friend?"

"Great, thanks. I'm really glad we could get together on short notice," Ryan said as he pulled out his notepad and pen, ready for another marathon note-taking session.

"Happy to help. I was pleased to see your e-mail. How is your V.P. doing for you?" Lenny winked. "It looked pretty good."

Ryan laughed wearily. "Boy, Lenny, when you said it was hard, you weren't kidding! The process of getting to our value proposition—one we could use, anyway—was about the hardest thing I've had to do at Wolfson. It was real work! I mean, getting everyone to buy in wasn't that difficult, since we all knew we had problems, but coming up with the right V.P. made me wonder if I wasn't in the wrong field!" Ryan shared with Lenny the process he had gone over in his mind on the train. "I tell you, Lenny, the hardest part was getting everyone to be objective about the whole thing. They'd all had their own ways of doing things for so long that it was tough to disconnect them from the way they'd been doing their work."

Lenny smiled knowingly. "I can completely relate. But it was worth it, right?"

"Oh, no question. Leads are up, and I feel like I have a new appreciation for how what we do is important to our clients. I'd always kind of felt like we were just selling furniture, albeit cool stuff for work and home office, but now I know what we're really selling, and it's very exciting. We're selling furniture that makes the buyer look prosperous and also keeps down work-related injuries."

"That's great," Lenny said. "So now you want to learn the process, right?"

"Absolutely," enthused Ryan.

"Good, good. Listen, Ryan, I'm happy to share the process with you, but there's no chance we'll have time to go through the whole thing today."

Ryan slumped a bit. Lenny saw his disappointment and hurried to reassure him. "But I want to make sure I teach you the whole process, so I was able to clear out my lunches for all of this week. If you're willing to come and meet me every day, I'll make sure we cover the whole thing."

Ryan was dubious. He had plans, after all. But with the success of the value proposition, he knew he was hooked and agreed. "Give me just a sec," he said to Lenny as he pulled out his BlackBerry. He checked his calendar and saw he was currently busy on three out of five days. He sighed and fired off an e-mail to his assistant Herta to change the appointments and block out the week's lunches. "Eleven o'clock each day, right?" he asked Lenny.

"Yes," Lenny responded. "I'll pick the restaurants and let you know where to meet me. We'll have a little kosher lunch tour of New York. It'll be fun."

"OK, Lenny, but take it easy on the vegetarian places. I'm a meat and potatoes guy. Kosher kills me—there's just no variety!"

"No problem, my friend. You are in capable culinary hands. So, how is your new V.P. working out with your staff and company?"

"Great! The CEO is happy, the salespeople are using it, and they seem excited about it. They're most excited about the increased leads and appointments—up twenty-five percent over last year! Still, even though we're getting in front of more clients . . ." Ryan trailed off and shrugged.

"Let me guess," Lenny smiled. "Lots of appointments, but the closing is still tough, right?"

"How did you know?"

"We struggled through the same thing. The V.P. is great for getting the messaging in synch. When the economy is hot, just that would have been enough to build a good business. But times have changed. People are careful with money today. They don't buy so easily."

"You're telling me!" Ryan sighed.

"The messaging is key," Lenny continued. "It attracts the right clients, but closes only the easy sales for you. In a tough economy it's not enough to just get business from your web site or the people who respond to your material. Your sales and marketing people now have to really sell.

"Think of sales and marketing like walking through a jungle. It's noisy, crowded, with everything attacking your senses. Somehow, some way, you have to break through all that noise and visual stimulation to get at the core of the customer. Get them to clarify the need and opportunity, amid the chaos of the jungle.

"When times were good and business was easy, everyone bought in spite of our communication. We only had to put the information out there in one way, and since there were lots of buyers, that was sufficient to attract enough of the easy ones. Now there aren't enough easy buyers anymore, so we have to find ways to appeal to all the various kinds of buyers out there."

"What do you mean *all* the buyers?" Ryan squeaked. He was beginning to feel overwhelmed.

"This is what I'm saying," explained Lenny. "Most sales and marketing people focus on the people who easily buy their products. Low-hanging fruit, if you will. Often they will test their message and sales process with current customers who are already friendly to the product. This has some value but leaves a lot of buyers off the table, buyers you need in a skinny market like today's. Now it's truly a numbers game.

"The trick is learning to sell to people who aren't easily convinced to buy your product. But these people have various different ways they need to be approached and convinced."

"What are you saying?" retorted Ryan, frustrated. "Of course, people are as different as the leaves on the trees in your jungle. But there has to be some way of finding a single common approach that can be effective. Otherwise sales and marketing people would have to develop hundreds of methods just to sell one product. And we have hundreds of products!"

"Well," sighed Lenny, "the bad news is that we have not found one single approach that works with everybody. However, we did discover—quite by accident—that four approaches would cover most situations."

"Four?" asked Ryan.

"Yes, we discovered there are basically four types of buyers."

"What are they?" Ryan was poised, ready to write.

Lenny leaned in. "Here they are:

The Wise Buyer
The Cynical Buyer
The Simple Buyer
The Buyer Unwilling to Ask

Ryan looked up when he finished writing. "This sounds oddly familiar. How did you come up with this?"

"We didn't," Lenny grinned. "Well, not exactly. Let's say we adapted it."

"Adapted it?" Ryan stared at Lenny. "From what?"

"From our ancestors," Lenny beamed. "Here, take a look." Lenny handed Ryan a tattered, thin black book. There was a page marked with a ribbon, and Ryan opened to it. He saw Hebrew on the right page and English on the left, as was typical in Jewish prayer books (which read from right to left) designed for Americans. He started reading the English to himself.

> Blessed is the One Who has given the Torah to His people Israel, Blessed is He. Concerning four sons does the Torah speak: a wise one, a wicked one, a simple one and one who does not know to ask.

Ryan's brain clicked. Slowly, he said, "I get it. This is the 3,500-year-old process."

Lenny clapped his hands with glee. "You like?"

Growing up in Livingston with many Jewish friends, Ryan had been to enough Passover Seders to know that the book in his hands was a Haggadah, the prayer book used at the Seder, and that this section of the service was where the people at the table would read about the apocryphal father who had four sons and how he was to educate them on the story of the Hebrews' flight from Egypt.

"I'm cautiously fascinated," Ryan said dryly.

Lenny sensed Ryan's apprehension. "Look, it makes perfect sense. Jews have been telling—or should I say 'selling'—this story of the Exodus since the days of Ramses in 1500 BCE. Through all the years and all the rabbis, they've stuck with the same methodology. You know what David Ben-Gurion said? 'Two Jews, three opinions.' You would think with all those Jews and all those opinions, if there was a better way to identify those who needed to be sold on an idea, someone would have mentioned it. Right?"

Ryan stared.

"Of course, right!" Lenny slammed his palm on the table in excitement. "Listen, Ryan. Golden Box has been using this for years and it's been amazing. We've tried this on hundreds of customers, and we haven't found anyone who doesn't fit one or a combination of these four types. Every time now our people can quickly identify which types we're dealing with and either close the sale or quickly determine when we are wasting our time. It's tripled our closing ratio!"

Ryan had to admit that whatever Golden Box was doing, it was apparently working. He wasn't sure he was ready to walk into the weekly management meeting at Wolfson and pass around Haggadahs, but at the very least he wanted to explore this concept some more.

"OK, Lenny, I'm game. Tell me how this works."

"Great! Let's order our food and we'll start today with the Wise Buyer."

Chapter 5

The Wise Buyer

Ryan stared at the Estihana menu. It didn't really look all that different than any other sushi menu he had seen. Granted, a few items were missing. No sign of giant clams or sweet shrimp, which was Ryan's favorite. "What were the kosher rules for fish?" He pondered. "Oh right, no shellfish. Something about needing fins and scales." He chuckled to himself as his overactive imagination immediately conjured up images of Finnish fishermen weighing large fish on scales. The waiter stood hovering and tapping his pencil. "Enough daydreaming," Ryan thought. He needed to order and get back to the conversation.

"I'll have miso soup and the Avenue J roll" (black pepper tuna, avocado with wasabi mayo and spicy crunchy salmon on top). "That should do it. Lenny?"

"I love your chicken udon!" exclaimed Lenny. "Great for a crisp fall day." The waiter wrote down the order and headed back to the kitchen, rolling his eyes.

"OK, Ryan, here's how this works," Lenny started. "Each type of customer needs to be communicated to in a certain way. The first trick is to *recognize* which type you're dealing with."

"Are you saying each customer fits into only one type?" Ryan asked, confused.

"No, of course not." Lenny shook his head. "Usually they're some blend of two or even three, but one type usually dominates during the interaction."

Ryan started writing.

"As I was saying, first you need to recognize them. Write down 'recognize the type,' OK? Good, so here are the traits of the Wise Buyer.

"First, you can tell that Wise Buyers have done their homework.

"The Wise Buyers may or may not be well educated, but they will read everything. They'll read every detail of your brochure and web site. They'll do Web research on your products and on your competitors' products as well.

"When they ask questions, the questions are based on facts they have discovered or that you have omitted from your material. Their questions are true questions without hidden agendas. And there will be lots of them. They may even have them written down.

"Wise Buyers don't get belligerent with their questions, but they are confident in asking them and the questions are deep and unemotional.

"Once you recognize the type, with any of these types of buyers, you need to *observe* the buying process from their perspective . . ."

"Wait, how do I recognize the others?" Ryan interrupted as he scribbled, "Observe from their perspective."

"We'll get to that. Let's stick with the Wise Buyer for the moment. I'll run down the whole thing with each one so you can see the process from start to finish. OK?"

Ryan scribbled madly and urged Lenny on. "Great, fine, go."

"OK," Lenny continued. "So like I said, you need to *observe* from the customer's perspective. The Wise Buyer's perspective toward buying is one of knowledge and curiosity. He or she . . . hmm, let's call this one a she. My wife is always pointing out (not without good reason!) how wise she is, in comparison to me anyway.

"As I was saying, she really wants, no, *needs* answers before she can make a decision. She trusts you to give her honest information, but she needs all of her questions answered. Until you answer all of the questions she believes can be answered, you'll never close a deal with her."

"Interesting," Ryan responded. "I've seen buyers like that. It seems like they're never satisfied with the information you provide and keep pushing for more."

"Exactly," Lenny replied. "Their entire outlook is colored by their need to make a decision based on knowledge rather than ignorance or emotion. Your challenge is to guide them toward a purchase, without pushing, even as their goal, intentional or not, is to ask questions until you drop from exhaustion."

"OK, so how do you close 'em?"

"Well, once you recognize them and observe from their perspective, you need to respond to them."

Ryan jumped in excitedly. "Well, of course. You need to respond . . ."

"But first you have to *acknowledge* their need to know," Lenny interrupted.

"Huh," Ryan said as he wrote, "Acknowledge concerns." "What do you mean *acknowledge*?"

"For you to gain trust and level the playing field, you have to show a buyer that you understand where she is coming from. Like in the value proposition, you need to show empathy."

"Again with the empathy." Ryan unconsciously echoed Lenny's newly acquired Yiddish accent as he said, slowly, "I think I get this. In both the value proposition and now this approach, you're working hard to connect with the buyer on a deeper personal level."

"Exactly!" Lenny slammed his hand down on the table again and almost sent his newly arrived udon flying. "You have to communicate to her that you want to meet her needs and you are trustworthy. You have to let her know that if she shares her concerns, you will do your best to *resolve* them. This is the fourth stage."

Ryan wrote, "Resolve needs" as Lenny continued.

"You need to give her what she needs to satisfy her curiosity. If you don't have the answers directly, be honest about it and then you can either get the answers later or work with the buyer to find the answers to her concerns."

"What if you can't find the answers?" Ryan asked.

"If you can't, you can't, but better to know that now . . ."

". . . than to wonder why you didn't make the sale," Ryan finished.

"Right. Hopefully you'll find the deal-breakers early in the process, but at least this way you're looking for them. Often, just the act of working with the Wise Buyer through the inquiry process will get her to buy based on her trust that one way or another you'll resolve her concerns eventually.

"She's wise. She doesn't expect you to have all the answers; she expects you to cater to her curiosity and her need to know."

"Wow! So that's it!"

"Just about. The four first words on the phrases you wrote down are the key," Lenny responded.

"Recognize, observe, acknowledge, and resolve." Ryan pondered, "Hmm, do you use this same four-stage approach with all four buyers?"

"Yes, the same approach works for all of them."

"How do you train your sales and marketing people to remember all this?"

"We use an acronym." Lenny smiled.

Ryan considered this for a moment and then wrote the words in a column, darkening the first letter.

Recognize the type.
Observe from their perspective.
Acknowledge concerns.
Resolve needs.

Roar . . . ROAR! Ryan roared like a lion and started chortling. "You've got to be kidding! How hokey is that!"

Lenny, a little annoyed, responded. "No, I am not kidding. In fact, that's exactly how we train our salespeople. It's become part of the culture. Didn't you notice the lion figurines on Courtney's and Gary's desks?"

"Well now that you mention it, yeah, but . . . really, ROAR? You've gotta admit, it's more than a little silly."

"Ryan, you want I should share this with you? Or not?" Lenny said, folding his arms.

"OK, OK." Ryan said, stifling his mirth.

"I know it's a bit 'out there,' but trust me, it works. Think about it. A roar will force you to respond, even in that busy, noisy jungle, right? Of course, right." Lenny continued.

"Now the trick is to keep the buyer from roaring back. There are things you can do that will just piss off the Wise Buyer."

"Like what?"

"Well, first, you can't just challenge her questions without basis. Remember, she's done her homework. If you try to argue with her without supporting facts you'll lose her trust."

"Makes sense. What else?"

"Don't try to sell her on emotional benefits. The Wise Buyer sees through this and will make her own emotional assessment. She'll likely see through the sales tactic and retreat.

"Finally, make sure your facts are accurate. Better to say 'I don't know' than to throw out guesses or, worse, provide inaccurate information. The Wise Buyer is sure to check your facts, and the second she detects dishonesty or carelessness, you've lost the sale.

"That also means your marketers have to be especially careful to not use absolutes that can be disproved."

Ryan surmised, "So, for example, I shouldn't have our collateral imply all our furniture is certified green if we still carry lines that aren't."

Lenny nodded. "Perfect example."

The waiter came over with green tea. Lenny poured and tried to sell Ryan on another course. "Ryan, you gotta try the dessert here. It's fabulous!"

"I don't know, Lenny. I'm watching the belly."

"Yeah I know. I'm watching mine grow, but these are great. Look, I'll order up one and we can share." He turned to the waiter. "Excuse me. Could you bring us a truffle dome with two spoons?" He turned back to Ryan to explain. "You'll love this. It's this chocolate truffle dome thing filled with a white liqueur-type sauce and topped with chocolate ganache. Yummy!"

"I can hardly wait," Ryan replied, loosening his belt.

The waiter returned almost immediately with the dessert and the spoons. Ryan and Lenny dug in.

Ryan looked at his notes and asked, "OK, so can you give me an example of a Wise Buyer?"

"Actually, I've been thinking about that. I can give you an example you would understand very well," Lenny replied.

"Go for it."

"Remember in eleventh grade, Mrs. Savad?"

"The math teacher?"

"Right. Remember when you wanted to create an Edison inventor's club and you couldn't get her to agree?"

"Yeah, I tried to persuade her and even tried to give her a petition from a bunch of us. I hounded her for several weeks with no luck. I tried to explain it was a good teaching opportunity, but got nowhere."

"Right, but you did finally win her over. What happened?"

Ryan looked blank. "Let me think. It was a long time ago, you know."

"Tell me about it. I can hardly remember five years ago these days, let alone more than twenty-five years!" Lenny replied.

"Uh . . . oh, right, I finally got her to let me start the club and we created some cool stuff."

"Did she agree easily?" Lenny asked.

"Not exactly. First I figured out she was never going to be satisfied until I changed my approach."

"Recognize. So what did you do?" Lenny asked.

Ryan, thinking carefully, replayed the interaction in his mind. "After the petition bombed, I went to her office and we had a meeting. I asked her what I had to do to make it happen. She expressed concern about cost and supervision and asked how we intended to resolve those issues. She told me her schedule was already full and there were budget cuts. I told her I was concerned I couldn't solve those problems and she suggested I might if I look at it from it from the standpoint of the faculty. At that point I tried to put myself in her shoes. And then I finally got it: I had to make supervision of the club into something that would add no significant burden to the teachers."

"Observe. You observed from her perspective how she was viewing the situation. You looked at it from her point of view."

"Yeah, I said I would try and meet her needs."

"Acknowledge. You were able to show empathy and gain her trust."

"I had to address her specific concerns, so I went back and found a way to integrate the club into an existing course. I got the other interested kids to agree to contribute money for materials and recruited two parents to share the supervisory load. I had them call her to discuss her participation. I put it all in a written proposal and brought it to her. I guess it answered all of her concerns."

"Resolve. You met her needs. So what happened?" asked Lenny.

"She finally gave in and actually supported me in creating the club."

"She didn't give in, Ryan. She bought in. You removed all of her obstacles and at the same time you engaged her in the process until she had a vested interest herself."

"Ahhh! I get it! I had to work her into the process, and I couldn't leave any question unsatisfied."

"Exactly!" Lenny exclaimed. "The Wise Buyer. ROAR."

"ROAR, right." Ryan pondered. "Hmm. I can even see where and how she roared back. I went in with incomplete information from her point of view, and she just shut me down until I came to see her side of the story and answered her needs. Pretty cool stuff, Lenny."

"I thought you might like it," Lenny grinned.

"Let's do the next one! What was it?" Ryan said excitedly, looking at the Haggadah. "Wicked?"

"Yes, but for our purposes there are no 'wicked' buyers. Just 'cynical' buyers. But listen, we're done with dessert, and I need to run. Let's save the Cynical Buyer for tomorrow's lunch."

Lenny dropped more twenties on the table and got up to leave. "Sit and relax with your tea, Ryan. I'll e-mail you tomorrow's meeting place in the morning."

"Thanks, Lenny! And thanks for lunch again. You really don't have to buy me lunch like this."

"It's my pleasure, Ryan. Consider it my mitzvah for the week." Lenny smiled and walked out the door.

Ryan sat sipping his tea and chuckled still at the ROAR concept. He knew it was a little childish, but he also knew he'd never forget it. That probably meant his sales and marketing people would probably remember it as well.

He paid the bill with Lenny's money, leaving a nice tip, and headed back to catch the Q train, roaring quietly to himself.

Chapter 6

The Cynical Buyer

LENNY looked around the restaurant and perused the menu. When he had e-mailed Ryan this morning, he suggested that they meet in Manhattan and that Ryan choose a restaurant. He figured they would end up at a kosher deli. This was no kosher deli.

Ryan could tell that Lenny was impressed with Mike's Bistro. It worked out perfectly. When Lenny e-mailed this morning, Ryan quickly texted his assistant to make reservations at a gourmet kosher place in upper Manhattan and Herta picked a beauty up on West 72nd.

Ryan smiled at Lenny and in his best New York Jewish accent asked Lenny, "You like?"

"Very much," said Lenny. "So many good things on the menu to pick. I like the name as well. Such a friendly name for a fancy place."

"Indeed. By the way, Lenny, this one is my treat. You've been paying for lunch *and* giving me this great information, and the guilt is killing me. You're doing all the sharing, here . . . is there anything I can do for you?"

"Oh, hey, it's my pleasure. I'm a big fan of this stuff, and I see it as a mitzvah to share. Plus it's a reason to reconnect," Lenny said, waving off Ryan's guilt. "It makes me happy to help. So, what are you having?"

"I thought the French veal chop sounded good. And you?"

"I have to go for an entrée-sized version of the hand-made duck gnocchi. I overheard some people leaving say it was the best gnocchi they'd ever had, kosher or not!" Lenny enthused.

The waiter came over and took the order. Ryan ordered quickly, eager to start the lesson. "So today we talk about the Cynical Buyer?"

"Exactly." Lenny started in. "Actually, this buyer is my favorite."

"Why's that?"

"Because once the Cynical Buyer is converted, he is the most loyal buyer of all."

"Really? Tell me more."

"In time. Let's start with our friendly lion." Lenny pulled a Golden Box lion with the clip out of his pocket and put it on the plate in front of Ryan.

"Ah yes, ROAR. Wait, is this for me, Lenny?"

"You like?"

"Very much! Thanks. Mind if I name him Lenny?" Ryan winked.

"Whatever you like," Lenny shrugged. "He should bring you only success. Anyway, let's start with 'recognize.'"

"Great," Ryan pulled out his notepad to start writing. "What are the traits of the Cynical Buyer?"

Lenny began. "He's fairly easy to identify. He trusts no one. He's one of those buyers who has his arms folded and who is sarcastic and stubborn. He can be insulting toward your business or industry. He's not necessarily mean, but it looks like there is a chip on his shoulder when it comes to being *sold*.

"The great thing about the Cynical Buyer is that you can tell he is engaged by how aggressive he is. The more he puts up a fight, the more interested he is—or the more he needs your product. Otherwise, he would just disengage and go away."

The waiter approached and set down the plates of food.

"Wow!" Lenny exclaimed. "This smells terrific. Who knew, a duck gnocchi. The only gnocchi I've had in the past few years was my wife's, which was good but not fabulous. Hmm, yours looks pretty good too."

"Yeah, not bad." Ryan took a whiff of the veal. Heavenly. Turning his attention back to the conversation, he mused, "Lenny, I think I know this type of buyer. He's not always rational with his questions like the Wise Buyer. Often he'll ask questions based on previous experiences, right?"

"Yes, exactly." Lenny paused to savor his gnocchi, then continued. "When you observe from his perspective you understand where those questions come from. See, the Cynical Buyer believes he's going to get screwed. Usually it's because he's been screwed before."

"Yeah, who hasn't?" Ryan commented. "But we're not out to screw him; we just want to make his life better, just like our V.P. says."

"Of course, but he doesn't know that," Lenny responded. "He automatically assumes he is going to be screwed by anyone and everyone. He has a general distrust of the way business is done and hates engaging in it for that reason. The Cynical Buyer is largely driven by fear."

"Huh! I hadn't seen these folks in this light," Ryan commented.

Lenny continued. "The first step for winning over the Cynical Buyer is to acknowledge his fear."

"Sounds like psychobabble, Lenny."

Lenny laughed. "Sometimes pop psychology isn't wrong. By telling him you're aware of his concerns about being mistreated, you start to build some trust. If you can get him to open up about his particular fears, you can make quick progress. Now, of course, you have to resolve his fears."

"Resolve, right. So what do you suggest?" Ryan asked.

Lenny responded, "The Cynical Buyer's needs are actually fairly easy to resolve. First you need to identify where his line of thinking may be inaccurate. Cynical Buyers are prone to generalizations, so it's fairly easy to pick out a concept he may have exaggerated.

"Here's where knowledge of your industry will help. Unlike the Wise Buyer, who wants you to facilitate her need to self-teach, the Cynical Buyer is looking for a trustworthy teacher. If you can teach him using facts that disprove his line of thinking, you'll get his attention and gain credibility in his eyes."

Ryan was writing furiously, "Teach and disprove, got it. OK, is that it?"

"No, not quite. Credibility is not enough for trust with a Cynical Buyer. You need to show sacrifice as well."

"What do you mean by *sacrifice*?"

"The credibility technique is your opening to help him see that you can put his interests first. Credibility brings him to the table. He's ready to be sold. But you haven't resolved his fear of getting screwed."

"Good point," Ryan conceded.

"That's why you have to show sacrifice," Lenny continued. "You want to somehow provide him with information or a concession that's blatantly not in your self-interest."

Ryan was puzzled. This seemed counter to sanity. "Can you give me an example?"

Lenny took a bite of duck and mushroom and closed his eyes for a moment, smiling to himself in enjoyment, before he spoke. "OK, let's say you have a Cynical Buyer who is concerned about your markup on the furniture you're selling. The Wise Buyer would have simply compared prices and researched the quality. The Cynical Buyer might instead say something like, 'I know you're making a ton off of me.'"

"Oh yeah, I've heard that before." Ryan laughed. "Too often."

"Who hasn't?" Lenny agreed. "So what you might do is actually pull out your wholesale price sheet and show them the markup"

Ryan choked on his water. "You're joking, right?! Then they'll want to negotiate the price!"

"Not necessarily," Lenny was emphatic. "The Cynical Buyer is usually pretty fair. They don't mind paying for a service; they just want to make sure they are getting treated fairly.

"If you show him the margin and logically justify the expenses associated with running the business and providing the service, you'll have educated him on the error in his judgment and he'll greatly appreciate the view behind the curtain."

"That . . ." Ryan was nearly speechless. "Um . . . That seems a little extreme."

"Well you asked for an example. I wanted to use an obvious one," Lenny countered. "Look, it doesn't always have to be quite so drastic. And, of course, you need to develop techniques among your salespeople that work with your company culture. Obviously, if you don't practice open book management with your salespeople, you may not be able to share that kind of information.

"But the point is you have to level the trust playing field. As soon as you show the Cynical Buyer that you're more interested in his needs than your own commission or secrets, you earn his trust and he's ready to work with you."

"Fascinating," Ryan commented. "It really makes sense when you think about it."

Lenny nodded. "The best part is that once you resolve a Cynical Buyer, he's the most loyal of all the buyers."

Ryan stopped writing, confused. "Why is that? I'd think I'd have to re-sell this guy every time I went back for another sale."

Lenny smiled. "Ah. No, remember you've just resolved his fear of being screwed—but only in this circumstance and only by you. You haven't cured him of his fear of being screwed by someone else. Now you have an advantage. He trusts you. He's too fearful of being screwed to try to find someone new he can trust. He doesn't want to get into the position of having to determine whether someone else is trustworthy.

"Ultimately the Cynical Buyer has difficulty trusting anyone because actually he doesn't trust himself to make the right decision."

"Ah, totally different from the Wise Buyer, who ultimately trusts only herself to find the right answers," Ryan added.

"Yes, the Wise Buyer will trust in the power of truth in vast repositories of information and in her own curiosity, whereas the Cynical Buyer has little faith in his ability to find the right answers. That's why he feels he needs to either have a salesperson to trust or at the least have one to blame if something goes wrong."

"Wow! That's a pretty cynical view," Ryan said.

"If the shoe fits," smiled Lenny. "You can see the distinction in these two buyers with online shopping."

"Seriously?"

"Yes," Lenny continued. "We've noticed that the Wise Buyer will do most of her homework online, and when satisfied, she will simply order online.

"In contrast, the Cynical Buyer will do some research online, but ultimately he wants to work with a live person to place the order and follow up. He craves the personal relationship. The higher the perceived risk to himself, the more personal attention he needs."

"Wait," Ryan interrupted. "Are you saying that a Cynical Buyer will never order online?" If Ryan was giving up a quarter of his online sales of home office furniture he wanted to know about it!

"No, but it's hard to establish the *initial* relationship without some *initial* human contact. Once the relationship is established, he may order regularly, but at that point, he acts less like the Cynical Buyer and more like the Simple Buyer, whom we'll talk about tomorrow."

"Can't wait. So I think I can guess, but what makes the Cynical Buyer roar back?" asked Ryan.

"Well, obviously, actually screwing him," Lenny smiled.

"Obviously." Ryan rolled his eyes and took another bite of veal.

"Truthfully, there's not a lot you can do beyond that to make him more upset than he already is. He's already created the worst scenario in his head, so as long as you don't live up to it you should be able to progress."

"The use of humor can help soften his attitude, although you have to be careful not to belittle his concerns by laughing at them. Usually if you cross the line and offend him, he'll simply disengage rather than do battle."

"Good to know," Ryan commented as he finished his lunch. Lenny's plate was scraped completely bare.

"That was superb. Shall we do dessert?" Lenny asked with a big grin.

"Lenny, I swear. Five lunches with you this week will have me gaining ten pounds."

Lenny looked at him with puppy dog eyes.

Ryan relented. "OK, fine. Let's share something. Do we need a menu?"

"Nope! I saw exactly what I want earlier," Lenny said excitedly. The waiter came around to clear the table, and Lenny requested the bananas tempura with praline ice cream and two spoons. Both Lenny and Ryan ordered coffee.

As the waiter returned to the kitchen, Ryan asked, "How can they have ice cream? I thought you can't have dairy in a meat restaurant."

Lenny responded. "I had it at another restaurant once. I'm pretty sure it was tofu-based, and it wasn't exactly ice cream, but it was excellent! I'm sure it's similar."

"Oh," said Ryan, deflated. Tofu in his dessert did not sound the least bit appealing.

Lenny sensed the disgust in Ryan's tone. "Trust me! You'll love it."

"Sure." Oddly enough, based on his previous tofu experiences, Ryan suddenly found himself feeling like the Cynical Buyer.

"Hey Lenny! I think I can identify a Cynical Buyer we both know."

"Really? Who?"

"How about your mom?"

The waiter placed the dessert and spoons on the table. Ryan thought it looked pretty good. Lenny dug in. "My mom, huh? Interesting, why do you bring her up?"

Putting a little of the dessert on his spoon, Ryan responded. "I remember when you first invited me over to your house in sixth grade. She was not very happy. I still have this image of her standing at the doorway as I left, arms folded and a scowl on her face." Ryan ate the bite and was pleasantly surprised. It wasn't Cold Stone Creamery, but it was pretty tasty.

As Ryan reached for another bite, Lenny smiled, perhaps because he had won over a Cynical Buyer, perhaps at the memory of his mother's reaction to Ryan. "Yeah, she wasn't big on the idea of me becoming friends with goyishe kids, gentiles, anyone who was not Jewish. Truth be told, she thought all the non-Jewish kids in town were troublemakers. And most of the Jewish kids, too, for that matter. There weren't a heck of a lot of religious families in the public school system. Yep, she was definitely the Cynical Buyer. Good call. Excellent recognition."

"Thanks. I won her over, though." Ryan grinned.

"Yes, you did." Lenny thought for a moment. "For the life of me I don't remember how."

"Really?" Ryan asked with raised eyebrows. "If I recall correctly, it was by helping you with science." Lenny suddenly felt adolescent unpleasantness encroaching on his culinary pleasure. "She was all concerned about your performance in seventh grade science and thought maybe I was distracting you."

"I vaguely remember . . ." Lenny played with his spoon.

"Yeah, well, I remember specifically that you were getting a D." Ryan chuckled. "I'm sure you've blocked out the tragedy. Anyway, she took me aside one day and expressed her concern and suggested in no uncertain terms that maybe I should give you some space so you would have more time to study."

"She did what?!" Lenny exclaimed.

"Yeah, it was a bit harsh, but I understood her concern for your grades. Or, as you would say, I observed the situation from her perspective. Since I didn't want to stop hanging out with you, I suggested an alternative. I told her that I got it, and that I knew grades were important to your family."

"Nice. Acknowledgment," Lenny said squirming a little uncomfortably.

Ryan continued, "So I offered to tutor you, since I was getting an A."

Lenny stared at Ryan. "Really!"

"Worse, I bet her I could get you to a C or better, and if I won she would allow me to come over anytime I wanted," Ryan said proudly.

"You bet her?! Hmm, you were craftier than I thought!" Lenny was now amused.

"Thank goodness you got a B," Ryan recalled. "How's that for resolve?"

Lenny slapped the table in delight. "Ha! No wonder she loved you after that. You were the only goy she didn't mind after grades came out that year."

"Yeah, well, I wish she'd remembered that when Miriam told her we were dating," Ryan groused.

"You know, mother-daughter dynamics are something special," Lenny mused.

They finished the dessert and to his surprise, Ryan discovered he'd eaten almost half of it. "Better than I'd suspected," he commented to Lenny as the check came. Ryan grabbed for the check, but Lenny was faster. Laughing, he paid the check with more twenties as Ryan sputtered uncomfortably.

"You can't win 'em all, Ryan. Listen, I have a meeting downtown in the afternoon tomorrow, so let's meet at a little deli I know on the Lower East Side."

"Deli! Great, finally a little traditional kosher food," Ryan joked. "Where is it?"

"It's at the corner of Grand and Clinton. 'The Original Noah's Ark Deli.'"

"Sounds good. I'll see you there at eleven. I'm looking forward to learning about the Simple Buyer."

They walked out together and shook hands before Ryan headed back to the office, relieved that the kosher meal tomorrow would be as simple as the buyer they would discuss.

Chapter 7

The Simple Buyer

RYAN arrived a little early at Noah's Ark Deli. It had been an easy subway ride downtown on the F train and just a short walk over from the Delancey Street station. He didn't often come to this area. Once in a while he would walk through it on his way to Chinatown. The narrow streets and the thought of thousands of immigrants living here at the turn of the century always fascinated him. He could imagine clothes hanging out the window and the hustle of street vendors. He had read it was a veritable melting pot of Jewish, Italian, and Irish immigrants. Now the Lower East Side was staid and almost featureless. Like much of Manhattan, it had gone upscale. Pity.

Ryan walked into the restaurant and was seated at a booth. He pulled out his pad of paper and was just about to review his notes when Lenny came in and slid into the booth across from Ryan.

"Sorry I'm late. I was at morning minyan—that's our daily prayer meeting—and another debate broke out over who wrote the Torah, or who transcribed it. Not that a debate is unusual, since it's our weekly discussion session, but today we had some of our most vehement partisans, so it went on much longer than usual. So, you had a good, relaxing evening, I trust?"

"Not bad," Ryan responded. "With two teenage boys in the house, *relaxing* is a relative term."

"I understand completely. Three kids do not make for a quiet home environment. We are blessed with everything but peace and quiet," Lenny said with a smile. "The girls are easier than my son, but when they fight, the walls shake and the chandeliers sway. Do you know what you're having?"

"I am all-in for a corned beef sandwich," replied Ryan, proud of himself for making a quick decision in fairly unfamiliar territory.

"Good choice," Lenny said. "I myself am ordering a specialty of the house. It's a potato knish stuffed with pastrami. I'll get some kishka to share as well."

"What's that?" Ryan asked.

"It's a beef intestine—actually these days it's usually synthetic unless you know where to go—stuffed with breading, smothered in gravy."

"Oh." Ryan made a face, unable to hide his discomfort at Lenny's description.

"Trust me, you'll love it!"

"I'm sure," Ryan replied underwhelmed. "Here's the waitress." Lenny ordered the food and a couple of Dr. Brown's Cel-Ray celery-flavored sodas, which he insisted Ryan try. The waitress left a tray of half sour pickles, and Lenny and Ryan set on to them immediately.

Ryan, crunching through a pickle, asked, "OK, enough of this chitchat. Tell me about the Simple Buyer."

"Ah, you're ready for more." Lenny smiled and collected his thoughts for a moment. "OK, now the Simple Buyer is very interesting. It's actually one of the broadest categories, but these customers can be the hardest to close."

"Really? Why is that?" Ryan asked.

"Simple Buyers are very clear on what they want, and either you can meet their needs or you are wasting your time."

"OK, so how do I recognize them?"

Lenny continued. "The Simple Buyer is very direct in asking for what she wants. She doesn't need or want a lot of information. She's probably either already done her homework to her own satisfaction or doesn't really care about the information in the first place.

"The Simple Buyer has specific objectives in mind. She knows almost exactly what she wants, and—often more important—she has a good idea of what she is willing to pay for it. Whereas the Wise Buyer has an insatiable appetite for information and will make a purchase only after she has complete information, the Simple Buyer is looking for a few pieces of specific information. If the information does not match her goals, she will not buy."

"Sounds like she's fairly straightforward to deal with."

"She can be," Lenny responded. "The challenge with the Simple Buyer is if her impressions are mistaken and you can't meet them, she'll walk right out the door. Unlike the Wise Buyer, she won't listen to you. She's already made up her mind."

Ryan considered this. "Yeah, now that you mention it, I've seen that type of buyer. Usually she'll come in and say, 'I know exactly what I want. What's the best price you can give me?'"

"Right, price may be her issue, or timing or color, or it could be other features. Even if she says it's price, or mentions a price, the issue may not be that specific price, per se. She might just want a deal or just the joy of haggling for price. Sometimes if it's a business customer (or a politician, oy!), she may be looking for a quid pro quo. Whatever her issue, she will identify it to herself and will communicate it to you as best as she can."

The waitress brought out the kishka. Ryan stared at the two round orange disks with their gravy blanket almost covering them. He had to admit, what it lacked in beauty it sure made up for in smell.

"Wonderful!" Lenny said at his first bite. He gestured that Ryan should partake. "You have to at least try a forkful!"

Ryan cautiously sank his fork into the weird substance and nibbled at it. It was warm and soft and tasted like a hearty stuffing. He popped the rest in his mouth, chewed, and said, "Hey, this stuff is pretty good."

"What, you thought I would steer you wrong?" Lenny mumbled, his mouth still full of kishka.

Ryan smiled. "OK, so what do I see when I observe from the Simple Buyer's perspective?"

"Simple!" Lenny leaned in. "The Simple Buyer knows what she wants. She wants what she wants, and she doesn't want to waste time or breath dealing with sales shtick. Truth be told, most of us are Simple Buyers for most of the things we buy."

"What do you mean?"

"Ryan, when you go to the grocery store, you mostly don't really need a sales process. The product companies already did that job on you through advertising and marketing. Or you know what you want because you've been buying the same item for years. You want a can of chicken soup, so you get a can of chicken soup. Simple Buyer.

"The only sales process going on that deviates might be, say, if you are buying fish for the evening. Maybe they have monkfish and you don't know from monkfish, so you start asking questions. Now you're the Wise Buyer. Or if you don't like supermarket fish because you don't think any of it is fresh, you might be the Cynical Buyer."

"I get it. It's not about the type of person, rather it's the way they're approaching that particular transaction."

"Exactly! Of course, when my wife goes to the store, she claims she is always being sold by my oldest. 'Buy me this; buy me that.'" Lenny mimicked his daughter.

Ryan laughed. "I feel your pain."

The waitress delivered the knish, which was practically bursting with pastrami, and the corned beef sandwich, which was easily six inches tall, and removed the kishka plate, which Lenny had cleaned quite nicely.

"Dig in," Lenny said excitedly as Ryan pondered how many trips to the gym it would take to work off this week's food fest.

"Not even sure where to start," Ryan commented, realizing that there was no way he could get his mouth around that sandwich.

Lenny left his knish on the plate as he went on. Ryan didn't know whether Lenny was actually getting full or was engaged in his teaching. "OK, so now that you've recognized and observed for the Simple Buyer, you have to acknowledge her, which is actually as simple as it sounds. Just make sure you tell her that you understand what she's looking for, whatever it is."

"What if you're wrong?" Ryan asked, corned beef hanging out the side of his mouth.

"No problem," Lenny said, sans corned beef. "The Simple Buyer will correct you immediately. But once you're clear, you should acknowledge the proper need."

"Makes sense." Ryan said, having finally gained the upper hand in his battle with his sandwich by eating enough of it to make it manageable. "I assume at that point I just resolve the issue by meeting her needs."

"For the most part," replied Lenny. "But with the Simple Buyer it's not always that simple. If you can't meet her needs on price or features, then you have to negotiate to a compromise. To do that, you may need to resort to Wise or Cynical Buyer techniques depending on how she reacts to being told 'no.' The trick is to make sure that both of you are clear on her needs and your ability to meet them."

"Huh! So buyers can change type midstream?" Ryan asked.

"Sure. Think about it. The client comes to you and tells you she needs a black Aeron chair, by tomorrow, and is willing to pay only $800. That's obviously the request of a Simple Buyer. Turns out you have a blue one in stock for $900 or you can order the black one and have it in a few days."

"Yep, that's my life all right," Ryan smiled.

"So first you tell her that you understand she wants a black chair for $800 tomorrow. Now you tell her the facts. You tell her you can get her a black chair from the factory in three days. It's $900 and that's the lowest you can do, but you have a blue one you can sell today for $850. Now the choice is hers, and she will make it. If she stays as the Simple Buyer, she will either take what you offer, choose to negotiate, or leave."

"Makes sense."

"But, she might change. She might ask what other kinds of chairs will meet her terms. At that point she is becoming the Wise Buyer and you can talk about the relative benefits of Aeron versus Humanscale or Steelcase. Or if she starts bellyaching that furniture stores are always a pain in the ass . . ."

". . . she's become the Cynical Buyer. I get it!" Ryan said excitedly. "So what makes her angry enough to roar?"

"Ah," Lenny answered, "one thing is not clearly acknowledging her need. The Simple Buyer hates having to repeat herself. The only thing that's worse is to ignore her need and try to sell her something else."

"You can't cross-sell the Simple Buyer?" Ryan asked.

"You can't hard sell her or try to substitute without the acknowledgment. She might be attracted by something else, but first you have to fill her burning need. Trying to get Simple Buyers to take something outside their need is like teaching a pig to sing."

"How's that?"

"It wastes your time and annoys the pig," Lenny said, straight-faced. "Remember when I went with you and your father to buy your first car?"

"How could I forget? It was a '68 Mustang. They wanted $1,200. I hounded Dad for weeks to go with me to the dealer to negotiate."

"I remember," Lenny continued. "Your dad knew you were interested in only that specific car, and he wasn't willing to pay more than $1,000. Simple Buyer."

"Right, but the salesman kept trying to suggest other cars and Dad wouldn't budge. I was thinking at one point he was going to just walk off the lot."

"Do you recall how angry your dad got? He got right up in the salesman's face and told him he had two minutes to take the deal at $1,000 or he was leaving."

"Uh huh," remembered Ryan. "I thought the salesman was going to wet himself. Hmm. I loved that car."

"It was a nice car," Lenny smiled.

"OK, your point is made. Acknowledge their need before trying to resolve it."

Lenny looked at his watch. "Ooh, Ryan, I gotta run."

"What! No dessert?" Ryan laughed.

"No time today, my friend." Lenny tossed some twenties on the table as he got up, grabbing a paper napkin and the remaining bit of knish to take with him. "Here, buy yourself some rugalah. I'll e-mail you in the morning with a place to meet."

Ryan frowned as he looked at the traitorous bills on the table. He'd really intended to pay the bill this time, but Lenny was just so quick on the draw! "Yeah, I'm looking forward to learning about the Buyer Unwilling to Ask. See you tomorrow at eleven, Lenny." Lenny was already halfway to the door.

Ryan asked for an order of rugalah, which turned out to be small chocolate and cinnamon pastries. He sat with his dessert and a cup of coffee, smiling, thinking fondly of his blue '68 Mustang.

Chapter 8

The Disinterested Buyer

RYAN received Lenny's e-mail early that morning. He was to meet Lenny way out past Prospect Park at some place on 13th between 46th and 47th. Ryan had never been to this part of Brooklyn before, as it was far from downtown. He picked up the D train at Bryant Park and rode for what seemed like forever to 50th street. It took nearly an hour to get to this area of Brooklyn. It was apparently a center for Hasidic Jews: they were everywhere! He felt a little out of place.

He found the restaurant. It had a plain name, Avenue Plaza Dining. In his e-mail Lenny had said it was a special favorite of his. Other than the fact that it was in a small hotel, Ryan didn't really notice anything special. He saw Lenny already seated at a table against the wall and went to join him.

"You made it!" Lenny exclaimed. "I was beginning to wonder."

Ryan shook Lenny's hand. "Yeah, quite a schlep," he said, using one of the words Lenny had taught him. It seemed so much more appropriate than "long trip."

Lenny laughed. "It'll be worth it. You'll love this place."

"So what's so special about it?" Ryan asked.

"Check out the menu," Lenny said.

Ryan looked at the menu. There were plenty of interesting dishes, including pasta, fish, even a chocolate soufflé—which he already figured had to be high on Lenny's list of choices.

"See anything missing?" Lenny asked excitedly.

Ryan thought for a moment. "There's no meat! This is a dairy restaurant," he said, proud of himself to have come to the right conclusion. "Not bad for a goy," he said boasting. "But I always thought of dairy restaurants as sissy vegetarian. It looks like there are some hearty dishes here."

"I figured it was time to burst that particular perception of yours," Lenny said. "You were unwilling to ask for dairy, so I found a way to present it to you."

"Nice segue," Ryan smiled.

"I like it," Lenny said proudly. "Let's decide what we want and then we can discuss the Buyer Unwilling to Ask, or as I like to refer to him, the Disinterested Buyer."

"Great, what do you recommend?" Ryan asked.

"We should really start with the potato pancakes. They're made from sweet potatoes with an apple and red onion compote, so they're not traditional latkes, but they're scrumptious!"

Ryan agreed that sounded pretty good.

Lenny continued. "I'm going to have the hickory smoked tuna steak. You might like the Jack Daniels salmon. I've had it. It's yummy. And, of course, I can't pass on the chocolate soufflé!" Ryan smiled in secret amusement. He had sized Lenny up perfectly.

Then he got serious. "Before we order," Ryan said, "I need to note that lunch is on me."

"We'll see," Lenny replied as the waiter came and took their order. Lenny ordered the soufflé with the lunch since he knew it would take a while to cook.

"So let me tell you about the Buyer Unwilling to Ask," started Lenny.

"The Disinterested Buyer," Ryan nodded as he pulled out his notepad and pen and started to write. "How do you recognize him?"

"The Disinterested Buyer," Lenny said, "is pretty easy to recognize, because essentially he has no connection to you or what you're presenting."

"Sounds a little obvious," Ryan said.

"This isn't rocket science," Lenny agreed. "As you know, there are many viable buyers out there who either are unaware of the value you bring or who seem uninterested."

"Of course, but you can't turn everyone into an interested buyer."

"No, of course not," Lenny responded. "But there are a good number of people who will happen across your locations or your web site, or meet one of your salespeople, who will identify with a need they didn't even know they had. Identifying them can be tricky, but it follows a certain logic.

"The trick is to figure out the profile of the customer who needs you but doesn't know it yet. For example, in my business it might be a product I buy that has plain packaging with little or nothing on it."

"I see," said Ryan. "In my business it might be an office I'm visiting where the reception furniture is worn."

"Exactly." Lenny continued. "Observing from their perspective can also be challenging. You need to identify the many reasons they might not be interested. Some may be general, like they just don't need your product or can't or choose not to afford your product. Of course, you're not really interested in engaging these buyers anyway. What you want to focus on are the buyers who would buy but are simply unaware of your value.

"They're hard to separate, so what you have to do is assume they are all interested and find efficient ways of flushing out the real buyers. This is where marketing really comes in."

The waiter interrupted with the pancakes. Ryan took a piece on his fork and popped it in his mouth. He chewed a moment. "Wow. These are great! Sweet potato. Great idea."

"I thought you'd like it here," Lenny smiled around his own mouthful of pancake. A little compote settled in his beard. Ryan pointed to it, and Lenny sheepishly wiped his beard clean with his napkin. "I was going to save that compote for dinner, but whatever," he joked lamely.

Lenny got back to his lesson. "So once you recognize and observe for these Disinterested Buyers, you need to acknowledge them. This can be a fun exercise in creativity. You want to find ways to get them excited about something they may consider unimportant. You need to come up with creative ways of focusing their attention on the problem at hand.

"This is why we use the No Naked Product concept in our marketing. It gets people who might not have noticed our products thinking about what we do."

"So getting their attention is the same as acknowledgment for this buyer?" Ryan asked.

"It resolves just as well. Your issue here is that they are disinterested. By distracting them from their current line of thought, you are basically acknowledging, 'Hey! You're not paying attention!' Once you get their attention and get them interested, then you have resolved their unwillingness to ask and they are now engaged."

"OK, I get it. So what happens then?" Ryan asked. "They haven't bought yet."

"Of course not," Lenny responded. "That's because once Disinterested Buyers become interested, they change into one of the other three types."

"What do you mean?" Ryan asked.

"Well, now they have engaged. How they act after that will be as a Wise, Cynical, or Simple Buyer. Oh, here's the food." The waiter removed the empty pancake plate and set down both of the fish dishes.

"Looks good, Lenny." Ryan took a tentative bite and smiled at the pleasure his salmon brought.

"I'm, like, *so* sorry I forced you to go to a dairy place," Lenny replied with mock sarcasm.

"Yeah, yeah, I concede. Dairy's a good choice," Ryan surrendered.

"Anyway," Lenny said, "back to the Buyer Unwilling to Ask. Here's a great example. You remember going after my little sister Miriam?"

"Oh, we're going there, are we?" Ryan raised an eyebrow.

"Well I figured it's an example you'd be—ahem—intimately familiar with," said Lenny.

Ryan feigned distress, rolling his eyes and putting the back of his hand to his head. "Fine, fine, stir up the painful high school memories, go ahead."

Lenny smiled in memory. "Miriam was the classic Disinterested Buyer."

"You're telling me," Ryan recalled. "I had a crush for a whole semester, and she didn't even know I was alive."

"Exactly," Lenny continued. "For one thing, you were my friend, so the thought didn't occur to her. For another, you were a senior and she was a junior. And, of course, you weren't Jewish. I mean, there weren't many kosher kids in the school, but you were under even that fairly low bar. But that didn't stop you from trying to get her attention. You obviously recognized that she was disinterested."

"That's true," Ryan replied. "I tried some pretty creative stuff to get her attention."

"Yeah, I think the best was when you stopped her on the way home from school and serenaded her with The Carpenters' 'Close To You.'" Lenny paused for effect. "On your trumpet." He snickered.

"Hey, it was the only romantic song we learned in band that year. I figured she didn't know I was alive in that way. Besides, it got her attention."

"My point exactly!" Lenny pounded the table. "You observed from her point of view. And what happened next?"

"In my own inimitably geeky teenager way, I told her I was interested in her. I think that shocked her more than the trumpet playing," Ryan said.

"Your playing was pretty shocking." Lenny snorted.

"Hey!"

Lenny held up his hands. "I'm just being honest."

"Anyway," Ryan continued, "I asked her out."

"Right, you acknowledged her lack of interest and resolved it by soliciting her engagement."

"No, just a date." Ryan chuckled.

"You know what I mean," Lenny sighed. "How did she respond?"

"She started asking me questions," Ryan said slowly, thinking back. "Lots of questions. What about her parents? What would Lenny think? So many questi . . ." Ryan stopped, comprehension dawning. "She became the Wise Buyer!"

"Yes! Exactly! Good thing you're better at sales than you are at the trumpet," Lenny quipped.

"Funny man," Ryan said. He paused for a moment trying to stop thinking about Miriam and focus on sales. "I get it now. Hey, what makes the Disinterested Buyer roar in anger?"

"Not much," Lenny responded. "They don't care enough to get mad unless you annoy the heck out of them. But if they didn't respond to your attention-getting tactics in a positive manner, they weren't likely to be real buyers anyway."

"I guess that makes sense," Ryan replied. He paused. "So that's it. All four buyers. And we haven't even had dessert yet. So what about tomorrow?

"Tomorrow I can't meet. I have a busy day, and I have to get ready for Shabbos in the evening."

Ryan knew Shabbos, or the Sabbath, was a big deal for many Jews, and especially for Hasidic ones. They didn't do any work from sundown Friday to sundown on Saturday. They had to cook all three meals Friday afternoon so that they wouldn't have to turn on the stove until Shabbos was over. Instead they engaged in a day of prayer and time spent with family and friends.

"Besides, we're not quite done yet," Lenny said. At that point the waiter cleared the table and brought in the soufflé.

"Beautiful!" Lenny exclaimed.

"I have to admit, it's a lovely sight," Ryan added.

"And smell." Lenny took a big whiff. "Let's dig in."

"Absolutely. So I'm confused. We've gone through all four buyers. What else is there to discuss?" Ryan carefully poked the top with a fork and savored a piece of the soufflé.

Lenny, who was already on his third bite, responded, "We need to talk about integration."

"You're a Hasid sitting here in a kosher restaurant with a WASP, who dated your sister, and you need to explain to me about integration?" Ryan said, grinning.

"You're hilarious," Lenny said in deadpan fashion and rolled his eyes. "As I was starting to say, working with these buyers isn't just a function of sales. It's a function of marketing as well."

"Everyone has different definitions for the two. How do you define the difference?" Ryan asked.

"Yeah, I know most people have no idea where marketing stops and sales picks up. We spent a long time creating our own interpretation. It wasn't that important whose definition we used as long as we defined the different roles and communicated it clearly in our company.

"In our company we look at sales as the interaction of our salesperson with potential buyers, from generating leads through closing and even handling the customer through the transaction. For us at Golden Box, it's where the two people connect."

"OK, I can buy that definition. What's the function of marketing?"

"We see marketing as creatively applying tools that make the sales process more efficient and scalable.

So, web sites, collateral—it's all created with the idea of helping the salespeople do what they do best to help the company grow."

"Interesting approach," Ryan frowned. That was not his view of marketing, which he'd always felt was sales' flashy—and profligate—sibling.

"Yeah, well, it might not be how everyone sees it, especially the B-schools, but it works for us. We wasted a lot of money, time, and resources on marketing that didn't have the specific purpose of supporting our sales process. The point is that now we've integrated both the value proposition and the 3,500-year-old process into our sales scripts and our marketing tools."

"So your web site caters specifically—individually—to all four buyers?" Ryan asked.

"Of course," Lenny replied. "Everything we do in sales and marketing we try to do with intent. Resources are too limited to do otherwise. We already discussed how the NoNakedProduct.com site helps engage the Disinterested Buyer. I assume you noticed how simple our home page is. It gets right to the point so the Simple Buyer can find the value proposition right there on the home page. But dig a little deeper and you'll find lots of stuff there for the Wise Buyer."

"Like what?" Ryan asked, thinking back to when he browsed Lenny's site.

"Our web site has more than fifty pages of material that is easily accessed based on what you're looking for. The Wise Buyer can see cost comparisons, product types, unique packaging solutions. . . . Anything we think the Wise Buyer will want, we find a way to put on the site with an easy way to access it. It makes us look smart to the Wise Buyer."

Ryan was scribbling furiously now. "How do you address the Cynical Buyer?"

"That was a little tricky to figure out. We now have a section on the site called 'Did you know?'"

"I saw that," Ryan recalled. "I thought it was interesting. There were a bunch of myths about packaging that you busted. Ah, I get it. Chances are, you'll show the Cynical Buyer that he is wrong and that you can be trusted."

"Exactly!" Lenny smiled.

"That's pretty tricky, Lenny! You guys really put some intelligence into this stuff."

"We're spending lots of money on people and collateral," Lenny said. "We don't want to waste any of it, so we put a lot of thought into the design. Just like we do with our product. We call it 'intentional marketing,' and it's been a real help to us in our sales efforts."

"Good point," Ryan said, as much to himself as to Lenny. He knew his collateral, his web site, and his sales scripts were not as well coordinated as they should be.

Some of the stuff they had was around from before he joined Wolfson. As a matter of fact, Ryan was suddenly convinced, his collateral was almost completely valueless. He'd seen customers throw it away even as he was leaving their offices too many times to have any misconceptions about that. He liked this concept of intentional marketing. He had a lot of work to do in that arena. Ryan sighed.

"Lenny," Ryan said, perking up, "I noticed that you don't have your value proposition laid out on the web site exactly like the plaque in your office. Why is it different?"

Lenny explained. "The V.P. language is a guide for our collateral. We often use various parts of it or variations to meet the specific objectives of the buyer we're trying to close.

"The key is to keep perspective. These are tools that will aid in closing. People can still be unpredictable. One person may be a combination of buyers, and your salesperson will have to ROAR appropriately as the person goes through the various personalities. And just because you ROAR, doesn't mean you might not have to ROAR more than once to close the sale.

"Not to mention, all the tools in the world won't work if you're not talking to real buyers. We work hard to focus our material on our target market. That's why it's an integral part of our V.P."

"I get it," Ryan responded. "These are tools for good sales and marketing people to use, but people are still people. I gotta say, though: you found some pretty good tools."

"Thanks," Lenny responded. "Anyway, you get the idea. OK, so *now* we're done!"

It turned out they were done with the soufflé as well.

"Listen, Lenny, I can't thank you enough for all your time and teaching."

"It's nothing. I want my friend to be successful, right?" Lenny said, changing the tone of the moment with a wink. "Besides, if you're a flop, it reflects badly on old LHS's alumni program."

"Nice," Ryan said sarcastically. "Hey, I gotta run, Len. It's more than an hour back to the office."

"Worth the trip, though, huh?" Lenny pointed to the empty soufflé dish.

"For the food and the learning," Ryan said emphatically as he stood up. He reached in his wallet and threw some twenties on the table.

"Oh, Ryan, don't you know your money's no good?" said Lenny, smirking. "The waiter already has his money. We're good to go." Lenny stood up as Ryan looked at him, mouth agape. Then he shrugged and put the bills back in his pocket as he rose. They both started heading for the door in silence.

Thinking about their discussion, Ryan mused, "Hey, Lenny . . ."

"Yeah?"

"How is Miriam?"

"She's doing great!" Lenny said as they walked outside. "She married a doctor, an internist, and moved to Cincinnati. Four smart teenagers, two sons and twin daughters. She's very happy."

"Oh, that's great," Ryan said, meaning it. He turned to shake Lenny's hand. "Thanks again for all of this."

"Eh! It was nothing," responded Lenny. "I had a fun week."

"Me too," said Ryan "Let's get together soon."

"Of course!" And with that Lenny walked off.

Chapter 9

The Referral

THE FOLLOWING SUNDAY EVENING, Ryan was relaxing with the boys, watching the Jets get pummeled. Ryan was tired. He had worked late most of the week integrating a lot of the 3,500-year-old process into Wolfson's new web site and sales pitch. They had made good progress, but it would take at least a few more months of work and training to get it all integrated. And the collateral was in terrible shape, as he'd figured. He'd made it a priority, and he and his staff had put together some good first drafts. He had something for each type of buyer, although it wasn't yet ready for prime time and certainly hadn't been tested on real buyers yet.

Ryan's BlackBerry began to buzz, making his side table vibrate. He usually tried not to respond on Sunday, but hey, duty calls, and in this market you need to be responsive. He picked up the BlackBerry and looked at it. It was a text from Lenny.

Ryan: Have I got an opportunity for you! I have a good
customer who needs furniture. I told them about Wolfson. They're interested. Can you meet tomorrow? Lenny

"That's a nice surprise!" Ryan thought. Good thing
he'd put a rush on that collateral! He quickly texted back:

Sure, len, where? What time?

The message from Lenny came back almost immediately:

Meet me at 1:00 P.M. @ 1372 Broadway (@ 38th). We'll
grab coffee, maybe a quick nosh and go together from
there.

"Garment district, hmm," Ryan said out loud to
himself. He replied back to Lenny:

C u there. Thx

"That was really nice of Lenny," Ryan thought. He fired
off an e-mail to Herta telling her to clear his schedule for
the afternoon. He knew she would take care of it first
thing in the morning.

Ryan normally didn't do sales calls himself and didn't
really expect to close the sale on the spot without any
up-front research, but he figured this could be a good
introduction and could be a fun way to test the 3,500-
year-old-process firsthand. At the very least he'd get a
good story out of it.

Chapter 10

The Sales Call

THE DAY WAS BLUSTERY. Ryan fought his way through the wind and blowing leaves to arrive at the meeting point, a restaurant (of course!) named Mr. Broadway. He walked in and saw Lenny seated at a table. Apparently he had already ordered. There were a few small plates of food on the table.

Lenny got up and shook Ryan's hand. "I ordered a few things for us while I waited since we don't have a lot of time."

"Sure," Ryan said. "What'd you get?

"Oh, a little of this and that." Lenny pointed. "A baba ganoush plate, some Moroccan cigars, and a little falafel. Just a nosh. Have some, and I'll tell you about the company we are meeting."

Ryan sat down and enjoyed a Moroccan cigar, which seemed to be a long piece of phyllo pastry wrapped around spiced ground lamb. "What sort of company is it?"

"It's called Sum Fun Learning. They're an educational software company," Lenny responded. "They've been my client for years. They make these great interactive programs that teach math to elementary and middle school kids. We do all of their packaging. They've been a good client. Now they're expanding their product line to include spelling. They've also been growing their online business, so I hope we get to keep working with them.

"The CEO is a very smart woman, Judy Walzer. B-school grad, she started the company from nothing. They've been growing nicely and have to do some expansion."

Lenny spent the next 15 minutes running down the history and his experience dealing with Judy and her company. Ryan sucked up the information and the baba ganoush. (He'd always loved eggplant.)

Lenny looked at his watch. "Ooh! We should go. The meeting is around the corner at 1:30. We have just enough time." Lenny stood up as Ryan looked around for the waitress. Lenny waved him off. "I already took care of the check. We're good to go." Ryan shook his head, amused at his inability to win the struggle for the check, as they threw on their coats and walked out of the restaurant into the windy fall day.

"So where are we going?" Ryan asked, struggling to be heard over the wind.

"Just around the corner," Lenny responded. "The address is 179 West 39th." They moved quickly to the calm of the building and checked in through security. The building was typical for the garment district. It had obviously been used for manufacturing at one time and was now carved into smaller office spaces. Like most older Manhattan buildings, it was not particularly fancy. Ryan reflected that the various parts of New York and its suburbs all had different flavors: the garment district was markedly different from the suburban business parks out near Ryan's home in Livingston, and Brooklyn and downtown Manhattan were like their own little worlds as well.

When they went into the Sum Fun Learning office on the twelfth floor, they were immediately greeted enthusiastically with a wave from the woman behind the front desk. "Lenny! It's been a while."

"Hi, Fran," Lenny responded with a smile. "Nice to see you. This is Ryan Miller from Wolfson Furnishings. Ryan, Fran is the one who keeps things running around here."

Fran, blushing slightly, said. "Nice to meet you, Ryan. They are waiting for you in the conference room, Lenny. I'll take you back."

Fran walked Lenny and Ryan back to the conference room. On the way Ryan noticed that the front part of the office was fairly crowded with cubicles. Some were fairly beat up. The cubicles didn't match in style or shape, resulting in a jumbled effect, with edges that didn't quite meet up and corners that had been left off cubicle walls. Ryan knew this look: companies that grew quickly typically had gone through several vendors, and never threw out anything, resulting in a hodgepodge of styles, finishes, and systems. Their existing furniture systems were good quality, although certainly not top-of-the-line. Glancing into some of the cubicles as they passed, Ryan noted the ergonomic issues: no mouse trays, unused and broken keyboard trays, monitors placed at unfortunate angles. The company was going to have a repetitive strain injury (RSI) problem in a few years. Ryan also noticed there was a space toward the back that looked like a fresh expansion.

They walked into the conference room and found an oblong table with eight chairs. ("Huh, three chair styles," thought Ryan.) At one end, farthest from the door, sat an attractive woman, likely in her late thirties, and a middle-aged man rifling through a stack of papers bound with a clip. Ryan assumed the woman was Judy Walzer as she stood and made her way around the table past the man and toward them. The man remained seated.

Judy and the man sitting with her were both dressed in business suits, which was common in New York City even at software companies. Ryan was glad he had made the decision to wear a tie, a look he typically avoided. But he had figured that next to Lenny's formal-looking black suit and crisp white shirt, he would look sloppy if he didn't ratchet up his normal dress. Besides, these were Lenny's clients and he wanted to make a good impression.

"Lenny, good to see you!" Judy did not offer to shake Lenny's hand. Obviously she knew that Hasidic men considered it inappropriate to have physical contact with women other than their wives and daughters.

"You as well, Judy. It's been a while. All is well with the family, I hope? I want you to meet Ryan Miller of Wolfson Furnishings." Ryan offered his hand, and Judy reached out and shook it.

"Nice to meet you, Ryan. This is our CFO, Vincent Chan." Vincent half-stood as he exchanged greetings with Ryan and Lenny, then sat down again.

Ryan and Lenny selected chairs, Lenny nearer his client and Ryan closer to the end of the table. They had started to sit when they heard talking outside the door. "No, just finish up that one section. I'll get back to you as soon as I'm done with this meeting." A young man in slacks and sport coat but no tie walked in to the room staring intently at his BlackBerry.

Judy introduced him. "This is Baldev Raman, our CTO." Handshakes all around.

"Sorry I'm late," Baldev said. "We are working on getting some bugs out of a new release, and it's been a little more trouble than expected." Baldev took a seat at the foot of the table, BlackBerry still in hand.

Judy took control of the meeting.

"So, Ryan, Lenny speaks very highly of you and your company. I had a chance to glance through your web site. I like that your products are certified green and ergonomic. We have been looking for that kind of product.

"None of us has much time to waste, so I'll get right to the point. We need ten workstations for our new expansion. Price is a factor, but so is service. We're looking for a long-term relationship with a supplier that can meet our needs as we grow.

"To be perfectly frank, we're not going to choose easily, but we want the choice to be a company that we don't have to think about and negotiate with every time we add a person or ten. And whatever deal we get from you now, I'll want to offer to my employees so that they can outfit their home offices. Make sense?"

"OK. That was pretty straightforward," Ryan thought.

As Ryan opened his mouth to respond, Vincent cut in. "I also had a chance to review your web site, Ryan. I liked much of what I saw. But found it lacking in some areas. I want to understand a little more about the process of how you choose your supplier companies and the warranties they give to support the servicing of the furniture long term."

"Great, Vincent. Let me grab a list of our manufacturers so we can discuss some of their specifics," Ryan said as he reached into his briefcase. He came back up with a file folder of small catalogs. When he looked up from his briefcase Lenny had put his notepad in front of Ryan with one word.

ROAR!

Ryan glanced at the paper and kicked into gear. He probably didn't need Lenny's reminder to remember the process, but it sure didn't hurt. First up, he thought, *recognize*. He dove back into his briefcase and grabbed the folders his team had put together to address the needs of the four buyers.

To give himself a moment to think, he turned to a quick delaying tactic. "Judy, Vincent, Baldev, thanks for agreeing to meet with me. I'm glad you got to see our web site."

Vincent had been to the web site and still had questions. That could make him a Wise Buyer. On the other hand, it was still too early to tell. He could just as well be setting up for the concerns of a Cynical Buyer.

Baldev was an unknown so far. He was so quiet, down at the foot of the table. Ryan decided he could safely ignore him—for now.

Looking at Judy's direct approach, she had to be a Simple Buyer. She got right to the point about what she wanted. *Observing* from her perspective was easy. She was busy, had specific plans in place, and didn't want to be bothered with the details once everything was set up. Fine. Let's start there with *acknowledgment*.

"I completely understand where you're coming from, Judy," Ryan said. "Our company is focused on relationship business. I get that you want to concentrate your efforts on the work at hand and that our role would be to take care of your needs from stem to stern and maintain fair prices in the process."

"Yes, exactly," Judy replied. "How can I be assured that I am paying fair prices and will not have to waste valuable time from my staff to get this done?"

There! Ryan saw his chance now to go in with *resolution*. "I'm not sure if you noticed, Judy, our section on the web site that discusses our Customer Relationship Guarantee. I have a printed copy here." Ryan handed her a copy.

"Can I also see that?" Vincent asked. Ryan handed a copy to Vincent as well, and gave a copy to Lenny when he noticed Lenny was craning to see the document as it passed him. Lenny leaned back, concentrating on the guarantee. Out of the corner of his eye, Ryan noticed that Baldev was busy on his BlackBerry and was ignoring the whole discussion. "Hmm," Ryan thought. "The Buyer Unwilling to Ask. Still safe to ignore him."

Ryan reengaged with Judy. "Notice we lay out our five-step process where we survey our prices with competitors and compare the benefits of the various products. Additionally, we assign you a specific qualified representative from our company who gets to know your company's inventory and will work with you to upgrade your inventory as it wears out. We take care of the whole process, including removing and properly disposing of the old stations and replacing them with up-to-date, ergonomic, environmentally friendly furniture that helps your employees feel better and be more productive. In some cases we can even give you a bit of credit for old workstations; we practice reuse where we can and have relationships with several organizations that refurbish and resell old furniture in poorer communities."

Judy looked through the material. "Yes, I liked how your company focuses on those issues. This seems pretty thorough."

"There is a sixty-day price guarantee as well, in case the manufacturer unexpectedly offers the product for clearance," Ryan added.

"This program has merit," Vincent said, looking up from the pages. "I would like to see more of the detail on the specs for each of the manufacturers you are working with and see how the durability compares to the price. Do you have that here? I couldn't find it on your web site."

"Ah," Ryan thought, recognizing Vincent as the Wise Buyer. Observing from Vincent's perspective, Ryan saw that Vincent felt an enormous responsibility to protect the company. Judy had placed her trust in him, and he would not—indeed, could not!—let her down, ever. Vincent had to trust Wolfson before he would let Ryan anywhere near Sum Fun.

Ryan immediately acknowledged Vincent's approach. "I completely understand your need for that information, Vincent. We keep it off the web site so competitors won't use our research. However, when I get back to the office I will send you a link to an internal site that has all that information. Once you have had a chance to review it, we can spend some time discussing it in detail and I can help you pick out the appropriate manufacturer and models for your needs.

"We can also look at your current terms on your existing furniture. As you may have read on our web site, we do a lot of self-financing and may be able to extend credit to help you upgrade some of the worn pieces I saw out there in a way that still fits in your budget."

"I would have to see more detail on something like that, but it sounds like it's a reasonable plan. It's worth exploring," Vincent responded. Ryan relaxed a little bit, feeling he had resolved Vincent's needs and knowing he had recently set up years of data comparisons on Wolfson's internal site just for Wise Buyers like Vincent. He heard tapping on a BlackBerry and abruptly remembered that Baldev had not said a word. Ryan knew that nobody in a sales meeting was unimportant, so he decided it was time to ROAR Baldev's way.

"Baldev, are there any specific concerns you have about this process?" Ryan asked, acknowledging Baldev's obvious lack of interest in the meeting.

"Huh?" Baldev looked up from his BlackBerry with a bit of a scowl. "Whatever these two decide will have to be fine," he said dismissively as he flicked his gaze back to his e-mail.

Ryan thought for a moment. He realized it was Baldev's people who would ultimately be using this furniture and who could make or break this relationship down the road.

"What will make this a good relationship for you?" Ryan dug again.

This time Baldev made eye contact with Ryan as he responded. "Look, I'll just go along. Every time we order new furniture, it turns out to be a real pain. So let's just get it done." In the silence that followed, Ryan could feel the intense attention the others in the room were paying to this conversation. Baldev obviously had some importance, and Ryan realized he could scuttle the deal before it had a chance to start.

Ryan recognized Baldev now as the Cynical Buyer and adjusted his approach. "I'm sorry to hear that. What's been the major problem?"

Baldev looked over at Ryan, put down the BlackBerry, and responded. "Well, since you asked, the last two times we bought furniture were disasters. The installers did a horrible job. The first time there were pieces missing when the shipment arrived, so we had to wait while the panels took up space. Then the next company didn't even install them properly, so they weren't sturdy and we had to keep calling to get them to come out and fix them. We couldn't use them in the meantime, so we just ended up with a big hit to our productivity. And now we're starting to get complaints about carpal tunnel and backaches, so it's clear we need to make some changes. We're in a damned-if-we-do, damned-if-we-don't situation."

Judy jumped in. "Oh, you're totally right, Baldev. The experience last time was just awful. I had to move out of my office, and I didn't get my workspace back for months. Hiring during that time was practically impossible; nobody wanted to work in an environment where people were camping out at Starbucks and McDonald's just to get the job done."

Vincent looked uncomfortable and frustrated. "It was totally my fault, Judy. I should have done more due diligence on those idiots. I called several of their clients, or at least people they claimed were their clients. What a bunch of crooks. And then they had the nerve to charge us for multiple visits to fix their screwups. I resolved it finally. It wasn't worth involving lawyers, but it still galls me."

"No, Vincent, it was that industry. I mean, they make a product you have to take on faith and trust them to do a good job. It's insane." Baldev pushed back from the table, exasperated at the memory. Lenny looked around, concerned, and seeming to want to bring the meeting back to a more equitable place.

Ryan surveyed the scene. The sale was going to fail if he couldn't fix the downward path the meeting was taking. He now faced a wall of Cynical Buyers: everyone had been converted by Baldev's recollections. He had to deal with the central issues, and fast.

"I get your frustration," Ryan said, observing from the executives' perspective. Then, in acknowledgment: "I can see how you would get frustrated from this process, and I see you care about your people." Sensing that Ryan really empathized with their issues, the group relaxed a bit and sat up, subtly changing posture as they listened intently.

"Here is some insight," Ryan said, beginning to work on resolving. "Many furniture sellers in the industry drop ship from the factory and hire independent installers, which can cause those kinds of problems.

"Over the years we've had those problems ourselves, but we've come up with processes to prevent them. First, we make sure that our installers are our full-time employees and have an average of fifteen years of experience. Second, we will ship your furniture to our warehouse and make sure all pieces are complete before we bring it over here for final installation. If you like, I can arrange to bring you over to inspect it all before we bring it here. You can meet the installers as well.

"We've also seen the results of bad installations in increased absenteeism from repetitive strain injury. So part of our process is to have an ergonomics expert evaluate the plan before we place the furniture order. We make the expert's report available to you to use in any litigation.

"And since you've had bad experiences in the past, and I don't want you to think the whole industry is rotten, I'll make sure we have an incentive to get it done right the first time. If we don't have it all up and working on the promised date of delivery, no excuses, I will eat the entire delivery and installation fee. No litigation necessary."

Baldev sat back in his seat, clearly impressed with the offer. "You'd do that?"

"Absolutely," Ryan responded. Lenny beamed.

"I'll want that in writing," Vincent interjected.

"No problem," Ryan responded.

Judy chuckled, responding to the change of tone in the room. "I like your friend here, Lenny."

"What, you think I wouldn't bring you quality?" Lenny grinned.

"This is good," Judy said. "Ryan, can you get with Vincent this week to put together a formal bid and selection? If it meets our numbers and needs we can likely place the order within days."

"Of course, Judy," Ryan responded. "Vincent, I'll send you over the e-mail I promised as soon as I get to my office this afternoon. If you'll send me the basic specs and the details of your existing furniture, I'll have one of my best people start preparing some comparisons."

"Sounds great. Let's get started!" Vincent said enthusiastically.

Everyone stood and the meeting was over. As he left, Ryan got a head bob and a little smile from Baldev, and that seemed to visibly relieve Judy and Vincent. Ryan and Lenny said goodbye to Fran as they walked out of the office.

As they were riding down the elevator, Lenny looked over at Ryan, who was quietly gloating to himself, and patted him on the back. "Good job! And especially well done noticing that Baldev was the most important decision maker in there."

Ryan glanced back at Lenny said, "Thanks!" And then he let out a little "Roar!"

Lenny smiled and acknowledged. "ROAR indeed."

Epilogue

The air had that fresh spring smell as Ryan sat outdoors looking down 45th Street toward Broadway. Lenny sat across from him, incongruous in his heavy clothing on this beautiful day.

"This place is pretty good, Lenny," Ryan mumbled as he took another bite of his wild salmon. He loved the tang of the balsamic vinegar and caper marinade. "This quinoa is delish!"

"I figured you'd like," Lenny responded, biting into his grilled snapper sandwich, a little red pepper aioli dripping in his beard. As he wiped up the aioli, he said,

"Now you know why they call the restaurant My Most Favorite Food."

"I think they got it right," Ryan responded. "I'm glad you were in the city today. Thanks for calling last minute."

"Sure, no problem," Lenny replied. "I know you've been busy lately, but I figured it would be a good chance to catch up."

"Yeah, but it's been a good busy. Everything has been humming. Sales are up. Pull-through is solid. I can't thank you enough for getting my head straight on our value proposition and ROAR."

"My pleasure. It's good things are going well. How's the family?"

"I gotta tell you a story about that, Lenny. Christina, my wife, had been having some issues at work. She felt like she hadn't been able to get the recognition she'd been looking for, and she was long overdue for a promotion. When she went to her boss to get one, he shot her down, being the classic Cynical Buyer. So when I started talking to her about the whole V.P. concept she thought it was fascinating and decided to do an assessment of herself to determine what her value was to the company. She took that to her boss with some thoughts on improving things, and poof, she's in charge of their marketing! It's much better money, and she is so excited."

"That's great, Ryan, congratulations!"

"Yep, we're thrilled. She's much happier and feeling more fulfilled in her job now. But wait, there's more. When we'd both learned about the four buyers, we shared the concept with our sons. Of course, my boys scoffed, but I noticed them trying out the approach on me. Every once in a while I realize what they're doing and call them on it. It actually makes them smile."

"I'm thrilled for you, Ryan," Lenny said. "The four buyers were based on the teachings of the Torah, and they don't call it the 'Good Book' for nothing."

"No kidding! Yeah, my younger son even laughed out loud once," Ryan said, tongue in cheek. "Anyway, the best news is that my oldest used the four buyers to understand the needs of some of his most difficult teachers. A Cynical Buyer teacher of his ended up giving him such a good reference, we're positive it helped him get into Georgetown! No scholarship, but we're looking at one of those up-front all-at-once tuition options. The younger one is thinking of applying early to three or four of the other Ivies. He'll get a merit scholarship, though, we think, if he doesn't go to an Ivy. Here's hoping, I guess. How about your family?"

"Well, the girls aren't quite ready for college yet, but they're kicking butt at school and on the soccer field, baseball diamond, and mall, respectively. My son's mostly keeping sane by staying out of their way," Lenny said. "And Sum Fun? How are my friends there doing for you?"

"They've turned into a pretty good client," Ryan replied. "We sealed the deal last fall and delivered as promised. Baldev was shocked. I put them in the hands of Steve, one of my best reps, and now Baldev calls him all the time. I think they've become friends. Meanwhile we've handled twenty new stations for them and replaced another ten. They're growing fast!"

"Excellent. Glad it worked out." Lenny smiled and signaled the waitress to bring the check. "Ryan, are you and your family busy next Thursday night?"

"I don't think so, let me look." Ryan pulled out his BlackBerry and checked his calendar. "Nope. All free. What's up?"

"It's Passover," Lenny said. "I would like you and your family to come to my home for a real Hasidic Seder. It would honor me."

"Really Lenny? I'm flattered. Will we understand it? It will all be in Hebrew, right?"

"Yes, but you're not the first guest we've ever had who didn't speak the language. We are happy to translate, and I have a bunch of Haggadot with transliterations and music so you can follow along with the songs. It would be a mitzvah to have you there. And I've been telling my wife about these lunches, and she's dying to meet the guy who can sit through more than one meal with me."

"We would love to," Ryan responded. "It will be a great cultural experience for the boys."

"Plus, Miriam and her husband and kids will be there. She's looking forward to catching up with you."

"That'll be nice," said Ryan. "I bet my sons get immediate crushes on her daughters. Isn't that always the way?"

Lenny nodded wryly as the waitress returned to the table with the bill. Lenny quickly grabbed the faux leather receipt folder and goggled when he realized there was a receipt instead of the expected bill inside. This time it was Ryan's turn to smirk as he snatched the folder out of Lenny's hand. "Actually, Lenny, I gave the restaurant my credit card before we even arrived here. Lunch is on me today."

Lenny roared with laughter. "Well done, my friend! Well done! So I'll e-mail you the address and details. You'll love the food. My wife's a fantastic chef. It'll be fun, there will be singing and laughing, everyone will get to participate. I have the perfect section for you to read," Lenny chuckled.

Ryan grinned. "Could it possibly have something to do with the four sons?"

Summary of *ROAR!* Concepts

For those of you who need a simplified outline of the concepts from the story or who just didn't have the patience to read the whole book to learn its lessons, we have provided a quick synopsis of the truths Lenny discovered and applied successfully in his business.

The V.P. of Sales and Marketing

Most companies do not communicate a clear and compelling value proposition to their customers. Messaging varies from salesperson to salesperson and is not supported by the company's marketing collateral and web site.

Even when the message is consistent, it typically identifies only features that have significance to the company—features that may be unimportant to the customer.

A compelling value proposition is just that, proposing something of value to customers in a way that will be irresistible for them and compel them to take action. The V.P. isn't always the exact wording used with a customer; rather it serves as the basis for all the copy used by your marketers in collateral as well as scripting for your sales force. Ultimately stories, pictures, media, slogans, and creative marketing approaches develop from the essence of the V.P. to compel customers to do business with you. V.P.s used in our story appear on pages 16 and 34 Other real-life examples can be found at www.jungleroar.com. The following sections discuss the necessary components for a compelling value proposition.

The Pain We Solve: *Empathy*

People often feel oversold today. Products and services are thrown at them, aimed at their *wants* with little regard for their *needs*. By focusing on the pain your buyers are feeling, you can connect with their true desire to resolve an issue. Stating their core pain will help them see that you understand what they are going through and identify you as someone who is looking out for their needs.

Understanding which potential customers are your best prospects is key to identifying the pain that will resonate with those prospects. Otherwise it will be difficult to tap into the raw emotional discourse causing their pain.

The pain statement should be narrow, specific, and true. An accurate pain statement reflected in your marketing materials not only will attract those customers who are desperately seeking resolution but will also repel those people who aren't really your customer, thereby creating great efficiency for your sales force.

The Best Solution: *Objectivity*

Once your prospect has identified with the pain you stated, you are 50 percent of the way to gaining a new customer. Now you have a perfect opportunity to show the customer how smart you are. The key in providing the ultimate solution is to hold back from selling him or her on you . . . just yet. By providing an objective way to solve the customer's problem, you keep the person's "Don't sell me!" defenses low, making it more likely that he or she will remain open to what you are saying. Providing objectivity in this phase allows you to build on the empathy and gain all-important trust with the potential customer. The solution you present must be simple and specific to the pain statement. It should feel like the most obvious solution in the world. If done well, the prospect should be saying, "YES! YES! Of course! Where can I get that?!"

Why We Are the Best Solution Provider:
Differentiation

In Lenny's and Ryan's examples, we outline three key differentiators that set them apart from their competitors. This should not be a list of features but rather your secret sauce that makes you special and unique. Once the prospect sees how in touch you are with their needs through empathy and how smart you are by suggesting the objective solution, the sales job is 90 percent done. But you can still lose the customer. At this point the customer wants to do business with you because you built trust by understanding what was needed and providing a solution. Now you need to close the deal by providing clear truthful statements, not sales hype, that helps the customer understand why you are the one to make that solution happen.

These statements should be tangible, provable, measurable, and difficult for your competitors to replicate. They will often include proprietary approaches and processes that only you can deliver. These statements are your chance to say to your competitors, "I double dog dare you to match this!" If they do, it should come at great expense.

This means you can't use statements that most of your competitors would normally use, because such statements would not truly reflect your competitive advantage—if your potential customers heard these statements from everyone, how can they trust that you are different? Here are some examples of popular supposed differentiators that really aren't quite kosher (we couldn't resist):

We have great customer service! Really, who doesn't say or believe they provide excellent customer service. This can't be measured easily against your competitors' claims. You can, however, create measured standards against which you dare your industry to compare. For example, if your customer service is largely by phone, you can tout your extremely short hold or resolution times or the amount of training your customer service people undergo.

We are very experienced! With the exception of new companies, most companies have experience at something. Often they total their employees' years of experience, making the number almost meaningless. Experience can mean something in highly consultative approaches, but it's how you apply the specific experience that really matters.

Our clients love us! Of course they do, or they wouldn't be your clients. The assumption is that unless you are performing services for your mother or your dog, most likely your current customers keep coming back because they appreciate what you provide. The point here is to tout tangible reasons those customers stick with you.

We are the low price leader! Maybe you are, but if you claim that's why people buy from you, the minute your potential customer finds a lower price you will be in trouble. Not only could you lose the customer, but now you also have a credibility problem. It's difficult to consistently back up an absolute claim such as this. Lenny solved this problem by giving volume as his reason for his competitive advantage in pricing.

We have never lost a client! OK, that's good so far, but the second you do for any reason you have to get rid of this differentiator. Not only will you have to change all of your collateral and web pages, but by doing so, you end up announcing to all of your constituency that you finally screwed up. Best to focus on those strengths that make for excellent client retention. We all lose clients, but it's not worth focusing your potential customers' attention on that fact.

We do it better! Better than what? Your competitor will never admit you do "it" (whatever "it" is) better than they do, and you can't prove it without establishing measurable proof. If you can establish measurable proof, tout the numbers, not just the blanket statement.

We deliver results! Of course you do. It's the rare company that delivers nothing and is paid for it. Instead of this obvious statement, be very specific about what you deliver. Detail the results that are most important to your customers or tie your compensation to the results in some way to prove your point.

Your statements must be true, measurable, and unique. Otherwise they won't have the compelling impact you need.

For more information on differentiating factors, we recommend additional material by Verne Harnish, the guru Lenny refers to in Chapter 2. Verne is *Fortune* magazine's "Growth Guy" and the founder of Gazelles (www.gazelles.com), and he calls these factors your "Brand Promise." Verne's book, *Mastering the Rockefeller Habits,* covers the Brand Promise in more detail.

The 3,500-Year-Old Process and Handling the Four Buyers

Gone are the days when you could put out a message and attract enough buyers of one type to make your business grow. Today you must learn to communicate to everyone so that you can accomplish your goals and maximize your success.

Fortunately, after many years of successful sales interactions, we can assure you that all buyers fall into one of only four categories outlined here. Taken from the Jewish Passover Seder, this identification of persuasion patterns has effectively communicated history and heritage for millennia. We have summarized the ROAR method with each of the four buyer types to make it easy for you to achieve ROARing prosperity.

Here is Lenny's ROAR approach for handling each of the four buyers:

Recognize the type.
Observe from their perspective.
Acknowledge concerns.
Resolve needs.

For each type of buyer, we'll give you a brief overview of the buyer, then we'll tell you how to implement Lenny's approach, without alienating that particular kind of buyer and making him or her roar back at you.

The Wise Buyer

Wise Buyers focus on making an unemotional decision based on facts so that they can be assured they did not make a foolish purchase.

Recognize the Type

- Wise Buyers need a lot of information.
- Wise Buyers ask many questions.
- Wise Buyers want the seller to satisfy their curiosity.

The Wise Buyer

Observe from Their Perspective

- Wise Buyers want truth.
- Wise Buyers are not in a hurry.
- Wise Buyers do not want to be impulsive.

Acknowledge Concerns

- Wise Buyers have a strong need to know.
- Tell Wise Buyers that all answers may not be available right away.
- Give Wise Buyers slow truths rather than fast lies or dissembling.

Resolve Needs

- Admit when you don't know.
- Be the Wise Buyer's guide.
- Partner with the Wise Buyer in finding the answers.

To Keep Wise Buyers from Roaring Back

- Do not pretend you know more than you do.
- Do not refuse to provide information.
- Do not try to sell on emotional benefits.

The Cynical Buyer

Cynical Buyers know they have been taken advantage of before, and believe they will be again. They are the most loyal of buyers once you earn their trust because they will believe they will be burned by others if they leave you.

Recognize the Type

The Cynical Buyer

- Cynical Buyers appear skeptical.
- Cynical Buyers cringe at being "sold."
- Cynical Buyers may appear stubborn, rude, or suspicious.

Observe from Their Perspective

- Cynical Buyers are fearful.
- Cynical Buyers have been burned before.
- Cynical Buyers don't trust easily.

Acknowledge Concerns

- Cynical Buyers have a strong regard for honesty.
- Cynical Buyers need time and proof to earn trust.
- Cynical Buyers' loyalty is yours to earn.

Resolve Needs

- Provide Cynical Buyers with behind-the-scenes information.

- Deliver on small immediate promises.
- Help Cynical Buyers understand how they're benefiting from your sacrifices.

To Keep Cynical Buyers from Roaring Back

- Do not belittle their concerns.
- Do not react defensively.
- Do not be secretive or obtuse.
- Never take advantage of them.

The Simple Buyer

Simple Buyers are straightforward and direct. They want something specific, and that's all they want, be it pricing, some kind of quid pro quo, or some other specific need. They will not waste their time with you if you don't correctly address their immediate need.

Recognize the Type

- Simple Buyers appear impatient and blunt.
- Simple Buyers are to-the-point and specific.
- Simple Buyers are nonresponsive to up-sell or hyperbole.

The Simple Buyer

Observe from Their Perspective

- Simple Buyers want what they want.
- Simple Buyers don't want to waste their time.
- Simple Buyers don't want to listen to pitches they consider useless.

Acknowledge Concerns

- Simple Buyers have a specific need.
- Simple Buyers are unwilling to accept compromise or variance.
- Simple Buyers need to know immediately whether you can service their need.

Resolve Needs

- Clarify the Simple Buyer's specific needs.
- Attempt to offer the Simple Buyer an acceptable compromise, if necessary.
- Disengage from the Simple Buyer if you can't deliver.

To Keep Simple Buyers from Roaring Back

- Do not overinform them.
- Do not underestimate their commitment to their stated need.
- Do not attempt a hard sell or a bait and switch.

The Disinterested Buyer

Disinterested Buyers, or Buyers Unwilling to Ask, are potential customers who are not aware of how your offering affects them. Once you get their attention, they will convert to the Wise Buyer, Simple Buyer, or Cynical Buyer.

The Disinterested Buyer

Recognize the Type

- Disinterested Buyers are paying no attention to you.
- Understand where your Disinterested Buyers exist.

Observe from Their Perspective

- Disinterested Buyers don't react to your marketing for a reason, a reason that you should be able to identify.
- Disinterested Buyers have environmental distractions you should address.

Acknowledge Concerns

- Creatively attract the attention of Disinterested Buyers.
- Be bold and loud with your message.

Resolve Needs

- Provide Disinterested Buyers with a clear and compelling value proposition.
- Prepare for Disinterested Buyers' to transition to another buyer type.

To Keep Disinterested Buyers from Roaring Back

- Do not ignore Disinterested Buyers.
- Do not assume you have Disinterested Buyers' full attention.
- Do not mistake Disinterested Buyers for people who are definitely not your customer.

Integrating the *ROAR!* Approach

The key to success for both the value proposition and the four buyers approach is to fully integrate them into your sales and marketing. What's the point of developing powerfully compelling messaging if your web site, collateral, and salespeople are all communicating different messages and are leaving out half the potential customers?

Management needs to commit time and resources to structuring the sales process around the value proposition. Marketing should be intentionally designed to bring efficiency to that sales process by communicating the V.P.

message in a compelling manner for each of the four buyers. Remember, all customers buy either because of the way you communicate or in spite of it. Better to get everyone and everything saying the same message.

Creating a Value Proposition That Truly Differentiates

Not everyone is lucky enough to have a friend like Lenny. You, however, now have something nearly as good: the story of Ryan's journey, told in what we hope is an energizing and entertaining manner.

Now that you understand the basics of the value proposition and ROARing to the four buyers, you can apply that knowledge to your business or personal life, increasing your success. Whether you are a CEO trying to improve the effectiveness of your marketing and sales force or an individual such as a recent college graduate communicating your value to a would-be employer, you will gain from the use of these techniques.

The critical goal, as Ryan learned, is to create a clear and compelling value proposition. This will require a commitment of time and resources in addition to input from several constituents. Management must be on board and invested in the project. If your company has significantly differing offerings or divisions you may need to create separate value propositions for those offerings or divisions.

Below is the four-stage process we use and recommend in our consulting practice to help companies establish their V.P. of Sales and Marketing and to help individuals create their own personal V.P.

Step 1—Gather Information

Some of what you need to know exists in the heads of your team members, but much of it your company is unaware of; otherwise you'd be communicating it already. Make a list of stakeholders in the company who interact with customers and talk to customers themselves. When we at TAE International work with a company, we talk to their competitors and target clients who have not bought from the company. Of course, we do this in a stealthy manner.

Talking to your current customers will tell you why people buy from you. It's often more important to talk to those who *don't* buy from you—this will tell you what your sales process is missing. As you might imagine, it is best to have someone unaffiliated with your company perform this survey so that they can get objective answers. When possible, we video part of the sessions to share key points with management in an unfiltered manner.

Employees in your organization who work closest with customers (such as salespeople and customer service people) can provide unrivaled customer viewpoints. Independent interviews of and research on existing and prospective customers can yield fruitful information. In all cases you'll want to perform a detailed interview that will lead you toward a successful discovery process.

For those of you creating your own personal V.P., you can use interviews with family, friends, teachers, employers, and mentors to help you learn about what value you bring to their lives.

Here is a list of sample questions that will help you in your search for data. Using these as a basis for conversation will help you drill down into the detail of responses. Do not use these as they are; customize them to fit your own needs. You can download these questions on a survey form at www.TheAwesomeExperience.com.

ROAR Interview Questions

INTERVIEW QUESTIONS FOR CURRENT CUSTOMERS

- What problems do we solve for you?
- What problems do we not solve for you?
- How do we perform better than our competitors?
- What do our competitors offer that we don't?

INTERVIEW QUESTIONS FOR POTENTIAL CUSTOMERS
(TO BE DONE VIA AN OBJECTIVE "MARKET SURVEY")

- What are you looking for but cannot find in the market?

- What are the most important qualities you require in a provider?
- What do you like most about your current provider?
- What would excite you enough to make you change providers?

INTERVIEW QUESTIONS FOR COMPETITORS

(TO BE DONE IN A STEALTH "SECRET SHOPPER" MANNER)

- What is unique about your product?
- Why are you better than your competitor? (Replace "competitor" with you, of course.)
- What, if anything, is better about your competitor? (You'll be surprised at the answers.)

INTERVIEW QUESTIONS FOR YOUR MARKETING PERSONNEL

- What do you believe is our competitive advantage?
- What is most compelling about what we do or offer?
- What is the most unique aspect of our company?

INTERVIEW QUESTIONS FOR YOUR SALES PERSONNEL

- Why do our clients buy from you?
- What do we offer that is different from our competitors?
- What do you sell that is different than the company's other sales people?

- What makes our product/service difficult to sell?
- What was your most challenging sale that you won?
- What was your most challenging sale that you lost?

INTERVIEW QUESTIONS FOR YOUR CUSTOMER SERVICE PERSONNEL

- What are the biggest complaints we receive from customers?
- What are the regular kudos we receive from customers?
- Tell me the story of the happiest customer you have had to deal with.
- Tell me the story of the unhappiest customer you have had to deal with.
- Which kinds of stories do you hear more often?
- Why do you think that is the case?
- What do you think we could offer that we don't?
- What do you think we are offering that is unnecessary?

INTERVIEW QUESTIONS FOR YOUR MANAGEMENT

- Which customers are least profitable for us and why?
- Which customers are most profitable for us and why?
- Are there enough of the profitable ones in the market to support our growth objectives?
- What is our competitive advantage in the market?

- What do our competitors do better?
- What can we offer that would be expensive or impossible for our competitors to replicate?

Once you have all the interview data, have a team member (see the following section) help you compile it into a condensed list, removing duplication and separating it into categories that reflect the questions you asked. This information will serve you well in Step 3.

Step 2—Select Your Team

We have found it best to select the team after the interviews because the interviews themselves will help identify those people who will be most helpful in the process. You need people on the team who can be objective and passionate and who have a stake in the process. It helps to pick people who have credibility and influence over others in your company even if—or especially because—they do not hold management positions.

Your team's size will range from 6 to 10 people. More than 12 can be very difficult to facilitate in a productive manner. We have identified below the roles that should be assigned. Not all team members need to play a specific role in the process, beyond contributing in the collaboration phase, but we have found in our practice that filling the roles below is critical to establishing a clear and compelling value proposition that everyone will accept and use.

Internal Champion: This is the leader of the process. This person has total accountability for driving the process forward and making sure management is on board. This person should recruit the team, set a schedule (not too ambitious—this process is about getting it done right, not fast), and motivate the team to meet the milestones.

Implementer: The Implementer is responsible for logistics. He or she should make sure all participants are familiar with the value proposition concept. (It goes without saying that the best way to do this is to buy each of them their own copy of *ROAR!* Volume discounts are available from many booksellers.) The Implementer should manage scheduling, disbursing materials, arranging the meeting spaces, and resolving conference technology issues if off-site people are involved. Often this person will transcribe the notes from the session, although another participant can handle this function at the sessions as long as the notes are distributed via the Implementer. Without the Implementer, the process has a tendency to fall apart, so choose the most responsible person you know and have that person keep the process in front of everyone.

Facilitator: The Facilitator will run the group sessions discussed in Step 3. It helps to bring in a professional from outside the company or division. Minimally, you need to find an uninvolved person with solid facilitation skills, who can bring out the information from each of the team members and maintain a productive yet passionate atmosphere, eliminating quiet politeness and allowing for creative conflict. Using an outsider in this role prevents the Facilitator from inserting his or her own agenda to the mix. This person must balance the roles of the Internal Champion, Objective Party, and Challenger with the other team members to maintain civil productivity and keep the process fun.

Objective Party: This person is the grand inquisitor of the group. The Objective Party's job is to make note or bring to the attention of the group or Facilitator when the group is beginning to believe their own brilliance. It's the job of the Objective Party to question, for example, whether or not customers would agree or whether competitors would actually react to the material the way the team thinks they will. This person should be somewhat academic, even pedantic, in his or her inquiry. It's this person's job to point out all of the implications packed into the statements being made, without advocating for change.

Challenger: Similar to the Objective Party, the Challenger is there to challenge the group-think consensus, to ensure that all aspects of the query have been covered. The Challenger should look at the opposite of the statements being made and advocate on the part of your competitors. This person does not need to be extremely vocal in this role all the time (which can lead to having staplers and the like hurled at him or her) but should strongly encourage the team to be aware of inconsistencies and potential dangers in heading a particular direction with the V.P.

Wordsmith: Find the writer in your company or enlist one from outside to help you craft statements that are powerful and meaningful. Every word in the V.P. counts. It will take a good writer to harness the words and create phrases that will have all the important ideas behind them. If you work with outside copywriters, bring one in for this process.

Participants: This is everyone else who will attend the meetings and voice their opinions in the group. They may at times act like Objective Parties or Challengers as they advocate for their point of view, which is fine. The important thing is to have a committed cross section of vocal and open stakeholders in the company who understand your business and customers.

Some people can fulfill multiple roles, if necessary. In our practice we often provide one consultant who can serve as the Facilitator, Objective Party, Challenger, and Wordsmith and work with the Internal Champion and Implementer at the company. Our consultants, however, are highly trained to perform all of these functions full-time, so when you are working with internal staff only, it's easier to limit each team member to a single role to keep each person focused on his or her specific objectives.

Step 3—Collaborate

Now it's time for the team to engage. The length of the meetings and specific agendas will be determined by your own productivity and progress with the help of the facilitator. Some teams can manage daylong marathons or even overnight retreats, whereas others find their brains hurting after only a few hours. Your productivity may also be affected by outside factors, such as work availability and proximity of the team members. The exact length of time is not important. Once you figure out how to work together, your Internal Champion can set milestones and meeting schedules that will provide the most productive output. Most of our clients find they gain immediate benefits from the process even before they are finished with the value proposition document.

The initial sessions are about making sure you have all the information. Begin by sharing all of the data from the interviews. Often this can be done electronically before the first meeting. Once the meetings begin, the implementer can provide updated notes, both after the sessions and a day or two before the next session. Let's face it. We all get distracted with our normal work, so this will help ensure that everyone is always up to speed.

Most groups start with either the pain statement or the differentiators. The obvious solution tends to follow naturally with one or the other. The best way to begin is to pick the one you think you are having the most trouble identifying and begin a group brainstorm on that subject.

Following is a sample inquiry form that we find helpful for the work sessions. You may want to add your own specific questions.

Empathy Questions—Pain

Your goal here is to really understand and articulate the pain of your ideal customer. If you can clearly articulate what they are feeling, when they encounter your company they will recognize your ability to understand and will respond with trust. Use these questions to help you and your company with the pain-understanding process.

- Who is the primary customer in your industry?
- What pain is that customer trying to resolve?
- What or where is the root cause of the pain?
- Why can't the customer solve its own pain?

Objectivity Questions—Solution

When you have successfully articulated the customer's pain, identifying you as an empathetic and trusted source, it's time to provide a solution. It should be an objective statement of your solution but should not include your features or benefits; those will come later. Use these questions to help yourself come up with the best articulation of your solution.

- What is the obvious "fantasy" or "ideal world" solution to the customer's pain?
- What aspects of the fantasy solution can be delivered in reality?
- What aspects of the solution can your company deliver?
- Why is yours a unique solution?

Differentiation Questions—How You Are the Best Solution Provider

Establishing your differentiation means coming up with at least three true and unique factors that differentiate you from your competition. These questions should help you find your uniqueness.

- What is your process for solving the problem and delivering this solution?
- What is your best competitor's process for solving the problem and delivering the solution?
- What can you do differently than your best competitor?
- What can you do that your best competitor can't do without great expense?

There is a second form on page 165 that will help give you perspective on what is being offered in your marketplace (Figure A.1).

Keep the discussion and phrasing loose. Often you will state ideas in one area (for example, pain) that will end up in another area (for example, differentiators). The idea is to make sure you have all the ideas and that nothing has been left out. **It is never important to finalize the wording in the room.** Wordsmithing during the session often results in an odd V.P. that few will buy into or remember. That said, it's beneficial to discuss and test words and phrases, provided nothing is set in stone. Often we will walk away with general concepts and proceed on Step 4 outside the group dynamic.

WHAT MOST COMPANIES OFFER AND MOST CLIENTS CARE ABOUT	WHAT ONLY OUR COMPANY OFFERS AND MOST CLIENTS CARE ABOUT
WHAT MOST COMPANIES OFFER AND ALMOST NO CLIENT CARES ABOUT	WHAT ALMOST NO COMPANY OFFERS AND MOST CLIENTS CARE ABOUT

Figure A.1: Establishing Our Differentiators

Step 4—Wordsmith Your Value Proposition

When the group is in agreement that all the concepts are accurate and compelling, it's time for your Wordsmith to get to work. Working with the Internal Champion, the Wordsmith should refine the concepts into clear phrases and send them out to the team for responses. It's important for the Internal Champion to retain ownership of the project at this point. It's the Internal Champion's job to get buy-in from the team. If the buy-in and understanding aren't there, it's time to head back into the sessions and let the team address the problems.

Once the pain, solution, and differentiators have been established, celebrate with a fun work session with the team to create and obtain a powerful URL that clearly states your compelling messaging and establishes attention in the marketplace.

In most cases, your value proposition will not be shared as written with your clients. Rather, it will serve as the foundation for collateral and scripting used to sell your company or product. You want it to be somewhat broad, because this will allow your salespeople and your collateral to drill down into supporting arguments based on each customer's inquiries.

Once you have identified the V.P., have your sales staff work to make it their own. They can embellish the main points with stories and examples to help the prospect connect with the power of the statement. You can take a similar approach with your web site by hyperlinking key phrases in the V.P. to case studies and supporting documents that emphasize your differentiation.

You will know you have it right when the value proposition is a comprehensive, truthful, and compelling introduction to your products or services that incites potential clients to dig deeper and repel parties that are not worth your efforts.

Integrating the ROAR (Four Buyers) Approach into Your Sales and Marketing

Sales people can easily adapt the ROAR strategy into their daily sales process. This book can serve as a training tool for teaching the process to groups or on an individual basis. Here are some ideas on how to incorporate the awareness and techniques associated with closing the Four Buyers into your company culture.

Discussion Sessions

The easiest way to help salespeople absorb the ROAR process is through group discussion. Conversations about buyers they know will present examples that can be shared and recognized. Once everyone has studied the summary, they should be encouraged to talk about the various buyers as part of the company culture. This discussion doesn't have to be only internal. In our experience, even customers delight in learning the concept and understanding which type of buyer they are in practice. It's usually a welcome part of *acknowledgment*.

Role-Playing

Not all salespeople are comfortable with role-playing exercises, but these exercises can be very useful. If role-playing is a regular part of your training program, you can design simple scenarios based on the four buyer types. Some people, us included, find role-playing uncomfortable. As an alternative, you can hire actors from a local college or community theater and write brief scenarios for them to act out with your salespeople, giving them a more realistic interaction. A fabulous resource for professional training of this type is the world famous Second City improvisational troupe. Their improv skill–based training allows salespeople to fail with buyers in a realistic but safe environment. And we all know we learn far more from our failures than from our successes. You can find them at: www.SecondCityCommunications.com.

Pop Quizzes

Unfortunately this brings back high school memories for us . . . and not particularly good ones. But preparing simple 10-question drill sheets that give buyer scenarios and ask for ROAR responses can be a simple and fun way of keeping the ROAR process at the forefront of your salespeople's minds. Of course, you can make it much more fun by handing out gold stars to the winners and offering big rewards for continuous success and improvements. Bottles of wine (*Manischewitz*, of course) and dinners out (find your local kosher digs) can be great theme-related incentives that encourage continual learning.

Self-Examination

Encourage your salespeople to recognize which buyer they represent in their own daily life. We all are each one of the four buyer types at some point. Have each salesperson share stories of how he or she was dealt with when acting as a Wise or Cynical Buyer. How did the person feel in the Simple Buyer scenario? When behaving as the Buyer Unwilling to Ask, what finally got his or her attention? By personalizing the buyers' perspective, they will be more attuned to the *observe* part of the process. Trainers can create games, exercises, and discussion opportunities that will bring greater empathy to the sales approach.

Life Story Sharing

Like Ryan, we have all had experiences in both our business and our personal lives where we either sold hard or were sold hard. Sometimes it worked, and sometimes it didn't.

Analyzing these experiences and discussing them with peers can trigger mental "Aha!" moments that will help provide knowledge and perspective for using the ROAR process. In those discussions, participants can determine how the ROAR approach worked, either successfully ending the encounter early or resulting in a finished sale.

Symbolism

Lenny was successful in keeping ROAR at the front of his employees' minds by putting a lion figurine on each employee's desk. As you may recall, it included a clip so that the V.P was at hand and seen constantly. There are other ways to keep these concepts in sight and mind. Simple laminated cards for the wallet are useful, as are posters with a lion and the ROAR concept. We have some of these items available on our web site (www.TheAwesomeExperience.com), but you can also easily create your own. Be creative in providing appropriately themed materials that casually remind your people how to ROAR. If you're technology-minded, you can download a ROAR app for your iPhone or iTouch. The important thing is to use the approach. The more you use the ROAR process, the more instinctive it will become.

Ultimately it is up to each individual salesperson to own and adapt the knowledge of working with the four buyers into his or her sales communication. Management can help make it consistent by examining and designing a consistent sales process that is replicable in the organization. With a clearly defined companywide sales process, marketing tools can be designed to achieve maximum efficiency and scalability for the company.

As we've noted, marketing's role is to provide efficiency and effectiveness to the four buyers sales process. The ROAR technique will work best when the needs of the four buyers are fully and intentionally integrated into your marketing. Most likely you will need to rewrite your sales collateral and electronic media (web sites, e-mail, text messaging, social media sites, etc.) to resolve the needs of the four buyers. Well-written and well-delivered messaging will resolve many customer issues even before you spend one minute of a salesperson's valuable time.

Here are some questions to ask—ones your marketing and sales both need to answer in the same way. Use these questions as discussion topics to incorporate into sales training, as well as to use as starters for marketing materials.

The Wise Buyer

- What critical information does the buyer need to know about your industry?
- What critical information does the buyer need to know about your product?

- What critical information does the buyer need to know about your company?
- What critical information does the buyer need to know about your competitors?
- What resources are available for self-study by the customer?
- What information or links can you provide electronically on your web site?
- How can you proactively put information in the customer's hands? (Consider books, learning events, seminars, etc.)

The Cynical Buyer

- How can customers be taken advantage of in your industry?
- How do you help your customer overcome the information disparity between providers and buyers?
- What industry secrets or insights can you share that your competitors won't share?
- What can you give up to ensure customer satisfaction?
- What absolute guarantee can you make about your product or service?
- How can you communicate this in your collateral and on your web site?

The Simple Buyer

- What are the key components to purchasing your product? (Consider price, specifications, installation time, systems, training, etc.)
- What are the boundaries in your offering? That is, what can't you offer?
- What is the simplest way to present your value proposition?
- How can you best communicate your value and boundaries in your collateral and on your web site?

The Disinterested Buyer

- What is fun or surprising about your product or industry?
- What is the little-known importance of your product and industry?
- How can you generate PR and buzz about your product?

With the answers to these questions in hand, put yourself in the role of each buyer as you examine your web site and collateral. If it doesn't work for you, it probably won't work for your potential customer, so, by all means, now is the time to be self-critical!

A sales and marketing dollar is a terrible thing to waste.

Giving Customers the Awesome Experience

Long-term growth of a customer base depends on giving your customers an experience that satisfies their requirements, is pleasant, and ultimately exceeds their expectations. We define The Awesome Experience as the convergence of *need, entertainment,* and *the unexpected.* Achieving The Awesome Experience isn't easy, but pursuing it is certainly worthwhile. To do this consistently, companies must master three components.

Establishing **compelling messaging** as taught in *ROAR!* is the first step to attracting, retaining, and growing your customers. By mastering *empathy*, *objectivity*, and *differentiation*, you will have the right message to communicate with any buyer type you encounter.

Applying **intentional marketing** to a clearly defined sales process will allow you to scale that process for growth. It won't happen by accident. You will need to apply *forethought, efficiency,* and *integration* to your marketing approach if you want to attract and close buyers effectively in a leveraged manner.

Providing **memorable delivery** to your buyers so that you stay at the front of their minds is the third component necessary for long-term customer growth. Creating a positive, lasting impression in their mind requires *creativity, intensity,* and *revelation* that leaves them with an "Aha!" moment, thereby permanently ingraining your experience into their life in such a positive way that they will desperately want to share it with others.

Although it's true that The Awesome Experience is nearly impossible to achieve in every customer encounter, without addressing and mastering compelling messaging, intentional marketing, and memorable delivery in your customer experience process, it will almost never occur. The specific steps for compelling messaging taught in *ROAR!* represent a good start.

There is more to come! As we develop more tools, we will release them on the web site:

www.TheAwesome Experience.com.

Please e-mail us at Kevin@awesomeroar.com if you have any questions or complaints or if you need advice. And, of course, if you need help implementing the processes, contact us!

Our Inspiration

In case you were curious: The Lenny character in the book is based on a real Lenny. Len Oppenheimer owns a packaging company and loves his lunches in New York. So much so he posts reviews regularly at www.LunchwithLenny.com.

The restaurants we mention throughout the book are also real places with yummy food. We had the pleasure of trying them all with Len. Following are brief Lunch with Lenny reviews on each.

El Gaucho Glatt
4102 18th Avenue
Brooklyn, NY 11218
(718) 438-3006

Glatt got your tongue? It will. Rustle up some friends and take a ride to the kosher soon-to-be classic, El Gaucho Glatt, where kosher cowboys meet the prairie for tastefully rustic Argentinean food.

I sallied forth into an appetizer of sliced cow tongue marinated in vinaigrette. Good tongue is hard to find. Maintain your standards; don't just jump at the first offer of tongue that comes your way. You'll be shocked at how good the Argentineans are at this. The perfect pairing with tongue is chorizo parrillero (beef sausage). Tongue and sausage—so right.

Head honcho Shmuel David explained that gauchos (cowboys) cooked their meals asado (barbecue) style, resting meat near a fire pit, allowing heat from the coals to slowly cook the meat. I grazed on a tasty tenderloin "steak a caballo," saddled with two fried eggs, mixed veggies, and tater fries.

The dishes come with various dipping sauces; the best by far was Shmuel's chimichurri sauce, made with garlic, parsley, and oil.

You can't ride off without dessert of flan and banana pancake.

Choosing my favorite dish was like picking between my favorite horse and my best dog. I need both on the prairie. Luckily this prairie is close to the subway.

Estihana
221 West 79th Street
New York, NY 10024
(212) 501-0393

We've all dabbled in "K," but a diet that's been popular for 5,000 years deserves a real try.

Estihana Asian Restaurant & Sushi fuses two seriously ancient cultures: Jewish and Japanese. Head Chef Ming Maidenbaum (seriously) puts the Shalom into the Shogun at this dynasty of a sushi bar. Ming's been kicking it kosher for 15 years and has perfected authentically Asian kosher cuisine.

We started with an udon noodle soup that may dethrone the venerable matzo ball. My bowl of bliss was jam-packed with taro, cabbage, onions, crookneck squash, various mushrooms, and chicken in a not-too-salty broth.

I wanted the rabbi of all rolls and was blessed with the Avenue J and Manhattan rolls. The Avenue J was seared pepper tuna wrapped with avocado, piled high with spicy salmon tartar, and dusted with Rice Krispies. The Manhattan roll (tuna, salmon, and avo, wrapped in rice, tempura-battered, and fried) was veddy, veddy interesting.

Words (Japanese or Hebrew) don't describe the flavor of General Ming's chicken, but my deep moaning sounds might.

Trust me and try it. You'll be praying for more.

Mike's Bistro
228 West 72nd Street
New York, NY 10023
(212) 799-3911

Mike's Bistro is a place where worlds collide. Fortunately, collision is pretty tasty. Kool kosher? Believe it! Mike makes it so. Here's the story: Mike, the owner and chef, was born in Italy . . . to Russian immigrant parents . . . en route to New York. Long story short, Yeshiva bocher Mike becomes an itinerant chef and, years later, reappears with a restaurant serving unbelievable contemporary international cuisine in NYC.

Joining us for dinner was a 6'4" Hasidic giant wearing a super bowl ring. Worlds collide again—it's Alan "Shlomo" Veingrad, former Dallas Cowboy and now Hasidic Jew/motivational speaker! Things were getting interesting and the food had not even appeared.

And what a treat when it did! We began with the Spicy Merguez Dumplings, which were delicious. Then the Baby Spinach Salad dressed in bacon, vinaigrette, egg, tomatoes, onions, chives. Yes you read it right . . . bacon! OK, so it was veal bacon, but fantastic. Although an appetizer, the Cassoulet (cranberry beans, white beans, smoked veal, duck confit, chicken sausage) was a perfect entrée for smaller appetites. The lamb was recommended; I figured the biblical sacrificial animal had to be something special to the chosen people. Keeping tradition paid off—my braised lamb shank was tender and flavorful atop a celery root and parsnip mash. My new kosher Cowboy friend Shlomo opted for fish. Chef Mike recommended the Walu Fish marinated with artichokes, peppers, beans, capers, lemon vinaigrette, and olive tapenade. He loved it. Good thing—you don't want to anger the biggest Hasidic dude on earth.

Dessert was Banana Tempura, delicious and not too sweet, plus a slice of pecan pie. Heaven.

This is the kind of meal you want right before you roam the desert for the next forty years. Check it out—www.mikesbistro.com.

Noah's Ark Deli
399 Grand Street
New York, NY 10002
(212) 674-2200

Maybe Noah was thinking lunch when he brought two of every animal aboard the ark. The best became deli meat at this very cool kosher eatery.

My ship set sail into appetizers—coleslaw, pickles, and stuffed derma (stuffed intestine filling made from meat, meal, and grain). If you haven't hit the deck yet, you're ready for the chai seas. For safety I ordered a knish stuffed with Rumanian pastrami and doused with spicy mustard.

Then my Titanic sandwich arrived. Pastrami, corned beef, chopped liver, and coleslaw, piled higher than Masada and resting between slices of rye. Saying a prayer, I unhinged my jaw to try to take a bite. My mouth was stretched to its limit, mandible cramping already upon me, then suddenly: a miracle! Moses appeared, cheering me on! Feeling no pain, my jaw dropped another three inches and the sandwich was in. The next miracle came insofar as I actually finished it.

With the black cherry soda's help I cleared room below decks for some fresh-baked dessert. Nothing says bon voyage like rugelach. This Jewish pastry is rolled with cinnamon, raisins, nuts, and chocolate. We finished the meal, and when the dove returned, we left the ark.

Avenue Plaza Dining
4624 13th Avenue
Brooklyn, NY 11219
(718) 552-3222

I judge books by their covers. That's just how I am.

Sometimes, however, books are missing their covers, and you want to dive in anyway. Plaza Avenue Dining such a book.

The steady stream of religious folks heading into and out of a basement caught my eye. And thank my lucky Jewish Stars, because this Brooklyn restaurant is a kosher dairy (no meat) gem hidden in the lower level of the Plaza Avenue Hotel. Lurking unseen below the surface is a bright and friendly staff and a highly entertaining owner.

I started with a Caesar but the Euro salad almost stole the day. Romaine, craisins, toasted almonds in a light, smooth dressing. Salad that's almost not a salad—now that's my kind of lettuce.

The extensive menu includes great creations that feel like meat dishes, not fish dishes. I was a little skeptical about the Buffalo Wings Style Tilapia, but after one taste I was hooked. Soft and tender on the inside, crispy on the outside, and smothered in a lightly spiced sauce. Actually a pretty good substitute for those messy little chicken wings. Lamb Chop Tuna was another fish dish in disguise. Juicy tuna medallions, sautéed in butter and served with tasty assorted dips. Outstanding.

The Jack Daniel's strips of salmon cooked in Plaza Avenue Dining's own maple bourbon sauce, accompanied by a generous helping of creamy mashed potatoes, had me thinking steak but eating fish. Even I, a Foodini (disguising one food to look like another) nonbeliever, had to see the light.

Plaza Avenue Dining doesn't have a liquor license, but they serve some decadent fruit cocktails topped with whipped cream and sugar sprinkles. We enjoyed the fruit punch flavor. Desert was even more decadent. Warm chocolate soufflé topped with ice cream, whipped cream, warm chocolate and side of raspberry sauce. What else can I say? It was a blood sugar bonanza.

Plaza Avenue Dining: Good food, fun staff, and everything disguised as something else.

Mr. Broadway
1372 Broadway # 1
New York, NY 10018
(212) 921-2152

Late afternoon. Siesta time, right? Wrong! Kosher joints don't sleep for nothing! We arrived, late, after the lunch rush but before even the early-diner seniors ventured out of their rent-controlled apartments. The service was fantastic—I thought I was at my mom's apartment again, but it smelled better.

Aperitif was some kosher pickles, brought out with extreme speed because they were just too good to keep in the kitchen. And did I mention how friendly the staff was? I couldn't get over it! We ordered rounds of baba ganoush, falafel, and Moroccan cigars, since we were only hungry enough to eat a horse, or should I say a camel?

What emerged from the kitchen was amazing for such light fare. The baba ganoush, so creamy and smoky, it could have been made from cream cheese whipped in a barbecue smoke pit instead of eggplant. The falafel was moist—you know you've got a strange food when "moist" is a desirable quality. And it was. This falafel, moist with the dew of a thousand chick-peas, and fried just the way I like it. Oh, and it went well with the not-too-garlicky hummus.

But the Moroccan cigars were the pièce de résis-tance! Crunchy but not hard, meaty but not beefy, this phylo-wrapped beef was exactly what the meal needed—some meat!

Mr. Broadway is in an unbeatable location, right downtown. Their menu rivals the best all-night diners of New Jersey—it's so large it needs its own zip code. Heck, they even have sushi!

Go! Go now!

My Most Favorite Food
120 West 45th Street
New York, NY 10036
(212) 997-5130

Picture your grandmother's fantastic, nothing-comes-closer-to-perfection cakes and cookies; the ones everyone says should be marketed. Think grandma's baking can hang with the best? First check out Doris Schechter's restaurant, aptly named "My Most Favorite Food." Doris was very kind—she could have named it "Better than Your Grandma's."

I raced through a good meal to get to dessert. Knowing what was in store for me calorie-wise, I opted for salad and salmon over quinoa. Really great, healthy food, but I was in a sugar daze, dreaming about the baked goods spread out on the counter right as you walk in. Salivatory marketing at its finest. I would've skipped right to dessert but I didn't want to embarrass myself.

Finally, the good stuff. . . peanut butter mousse cake, take-me-back-to-my-childhood and stick-to-the-roof-of-my-mouth kind of peanut butter memories. Carrot cake that will have you looking at the orange root in a whole new light. Cheese cake so good, I skipped my lactose pills. Strawberry shortcake that comes with flashbacks to elementary school birthday parties. Then, without warning, something called grandmother's apple cake. Apples so perfect and a crust so thick that I felt my grandmother's presence. We are talking an out-of-body dessert experience here. Then the sugar took hold and that's all I can remember. I regained consciousness about a week later.

This place takes the cake with a 5 Stars-of-David rating.

Acknowledgments

The authors would like to thank:

- Peter Economy for his insistence and coaching;
- Sam Horn, author of *POP! Stand Out in Any Crowd,* for her help with the title;
- Len Oppenheimer for his inspiration;
- Manish Chandra for teaching the value of empathy in business;
- Our families for their love and patience;
- Our agent, Joy Tutela, for her tolerance;
- TCG, for being good sports and excellent guinea pigs;
- Judith A. Turner, for doing a crackerjack editing job on both this book and on a fantastic Haggadah;
- Spencer Daum, who can draw better than both of us put together, for his drawings of the four buyers.

- Our Editor, Richard Narramore, and all of the helpful people at Wiley, for giving us a legitimate shot at the Jewish Super Bowl ring.

- And the many friends, Gazelles, and EOers who gave their feedback and support in the development of this book.

About the Authors

Kevin Daum

Kevin Daum is an author, marketer, and Inc. 500 entrepreneur. Kevin's sales and marketing approach resulted in more than $1 billion in sales with a 95 percent pull-through rate. His books include *What the Banks Won't Tell You* (Grady Parsons) and *Building Your Own Home for Dummies* (Wiley). He addresses the "green" customer experience in his forthcoming book *Green$ense: Rating the Real Payoff from 50 Green Home Projects* (Taunton).

Leveraging his degree and background in Theatre Arts, Kevin has built several successful companies. Most recently he founded TAE International, helping corporations pursue The Awesome Experience through compelling messaging, intentional marketing, and memorable delivery. He regularly publishes articles and speaks on the relationship between arts and business, customer experience, and creativity.

Kevin is a graduate of the MIT Entrepreneurial Executive Leadership program and a longtime member of the Entrepreneurs' Organization, having held several board positions. Kevin designed, produced, and led award-winning executive and entrepreneur training programs on four continents. Named one of the "40 people under 40" to watch in San Francisco, Kevin was named Distinguished Alum by his alma mater, Humboldt State University.

Kevin is the national columnist for *Smart Business* magazine (www.sbonline.com) and can be reached at Kevin@TheAwesomeExperience.com.

Daniel A. Turner

Daniel A. Turner is President of Turner Consulting Group, Inc. A graduate of Rutgers University with degrees in Computer Science and Creative Writing, Dan formed TCG in 1994, immediately after college at the dawn of the Internet era, as a new kind of organization based on distributed applications development using object-oriented design and methodology-driven processes.

An Inc. 500 and two-time Inc. 5000 company, TCG focuses on grants management, grantee community creation, and management consulting. TCG has worked extensively for several divisions of the National Institutes of Health, the National Science Foundation, the U.S. Department of Agriculture, the Department of Justice, and the Department of Transportation, as well as for private industry. One of their projects, iEdison (www.iedison.gov), won a Hammer award for government reinvention from then-Vice President Al Gore.

Dan is on the board of the Entrepreneurs' Organization's (EO) Washington, DC, chapter and organizes and travels extensively to EO events worldwide.

When he is not building TCG, Dan gazes lovingly into the eyes of his wife, Allison, and dotes on his daughter, Miriam. When he can tear himself away, he buys copies of *Story Number 1* and *Story Number 2,* by Eugene Ionesco (illustrated by Etienne Delessert), and his favorite business book, *How to Become King,* by Jan Terlouw.

Bonus Chapter

Bob Bryant was on a rant.

"Christina, you want to go into marketing? Are you kidding? You're a pretty good underwriter, but you'd make a crappy marketing rep. You don't know the first thing about marketing! None of you underwriters do! You think you're all good at understanding the clients because you talk to them every so often, but when you get into the sales and marketing world you just freeze up. You're like robots! Seriously, you need to be thinking about how you can increase your throughput, not day-dreaming about marketing."

Christina quailed under Bob's attack. She was stunned. She knew she wasn't really making the numbers that Bob had set, but none of the underwriters were as fast as he wanted. And she knew she could do better as a marketing representative.

"But Bob, I was just thinking that maybe I would be able to serve the company better . . ."

"Cassidy Mutual Insurance will be best served by you doing the job you were hired to do. You're a smart lady. Take a look around! We're getting killed on our margins, our overhead is too high, and customers are dropping like flies. We've already done two rounds of layoffs. The board is on my back to do another round." Bob stood up, came around to Christina's side of the desk, and leaned back against it in front of her. "Look, I know you're hard-working. And you really seem to care about our customers. You're a fine underwriter. Why don't you try to hone those skills and we'll talk about moving you to marketing in a couple of years when the economy improves a little, OK?"

Christina left Bob's office crushed. She didn't under-stand what had happened, but she knew there was no chance of her getting a promotion this year. She wasn't even getting a cost-of-living raise. He'd said she was lucky he was keeping her at the same salary rather than low-ering it. The rest of the day she went about her job mechanically, and all the way home the pretty fall colors didn't distract her from going over the meeting again and again in her mind. She hoped Ryan would be home on time this evening; she wanted to talk to him about the meeting. He'd been putting in really long hours for the past few months.

Happily, Ryan's car was in the garage when she got there. When she went inside, he took one look at her and steered her into the living room to have a seat; then he went to the fridge to get two beers. "You look like you need this," he said, offering her one.

"Oh, you have no idea, Ryan," Christina sighed. "I had my annual review today and brought up the idea of my going into marketing."

"Didn't go well, eh?"

"Not at all, no. Bob was in rare form today, ranting and raving about how underwriters make terrible marketing reps. I feel like he doesn't really understand how good a job I'm doing, and I don't know how to make him get it. Plus the company's in trouble."

Ryan winced. "Are they talking about another round of layoffs?"

"Yeah. It sucks."

Christina and Ryan sat and drank their beers in silence for a minute.

"You know," Ryan said, breaking their reverie. "I've been doing this V.P. thing at work for the past few months."

"Sure, that process Lenny taught you. I take it from your early arrival home that you're almost done?"

"Totally done! In fact, I sent off my V.P. to Lenny this afternoon and we've set up lunch for Monday for him to tell me that 3,500-year-old secret he mentioned. Here, I'll give you a copy of our V.P."

Ryan went to his briefcase and came back with a laminated card with his V.P. on it. Christina read the card and looked at Ryan. "This is pretty good! Terse, pithy, it describes Wolfson exactly! Cool URL, too."

"Thanks! So I was thinking that the process of coming up with the V.P. might be good for you to do on yourself. It'll certainly up your confidence level when you talk to Bob again."

Christina looked dubious. "Uh, right. So (a) I don't know how to do that, and (b) didn't this take you, like, four months to put together?"

"Well, to (b), it only took three months, and I had a lot more people to convince. You have only one person. I bet you could do it this weekend. And to (a), I'm happy to coach you along the way. Couldn't hurt, right? Kind of like you coached me through being a Little League coach. I needed the help, that's for sure!"

Christina remembered the arguments they'd had about how best to run a team consisting of kids who weren't in it to win but really just wanted to enjoy the game.

The outcome had been really good—they'd made it to the regional semifinals, and the kids had been thrilled. Even most of the other parents had been happy. And Christina had been able to stop coaching the team herself, which made her ecstatic.

"All right, I'm game. Let's try it."

Over the weekend, while their sons were alternately studying, playing with their game consoles, and studiously ignoring them, Ryan and Christina went through the process of determining Cassidy's (and Bob's) pain. Ultimately it looked like the industry was going through some major changes, and being a low-cost provider was getting Cassidy involved in a "race to the bottom"—every year their margins were getting smaller and smaller, while their costs were staying the same or increasing. The obvious solution was to make more money on every client. The sticky point came when Christina had to figure out why she was the best solution provider.

"I just don't know how I can be the one to fix this, Ryan. I mean, I don't have any experience with marketing, and this is almost definitely a job for an expert."

"You *are* an expert!" Ryan said emphatically. "What did you do for the LSO? Didn't you increase all their metrics? Didn't they give you an award?"

It was true, Christina reflected. Her boys had occasionally competed in the Livingston Symphony Orchestra's

Young Artist Concerto Competitions, and Christina had realized she really enjoyed talking about the orchestra.

At the end of the 2006 season, she'd approached the LSO and presented her case. "You need to increase your attendance and don't have the money to hire another marketing person. You need someone who will volunteer and dedicate themselves to your cause.

"I'm intelligent and hard-working, and I'll work for nothing. My goal is to improve your visibility in the community, driving seat sales and increasing small donations, since small donors turn into big ones later. I have a ton of connections in town, both through my husband's family and through my own connections with other parents. I'm willing to put the work in and I have creative ideas."

The LSO had had success with other volunteers who'd suggested marketing would be their forte, so they were willing to try her out. When the next season started their butt-in-seat metric was up by 15 percent and her "Beats on the Street" marketing plan had come to a crescendo with a full 40 percent of Livingston residents knowing about their offerings. And there were signs that donations would be up substantially. Christina was given the fairly prestigious "Volunteer of the Year" award by the LSO the following year.

"So my differentiators are the smarts, the skills, and the knowledge of our industry to get it all done."

"I'd hire you," Ryan said with a grin.

On Monday Christina went into the office with a plan. She used Bob's much-touted "open door policy" to ask him if she could talk to him about her annual review. He agreed that they'd meet a week from that day but also noted that there was nothing he could do about her lack of a raise or a promotion. She nodded and thanked him for the opportunity anyway.

That night Ryan came home so excited he was practically buzzing. His lunch with Lenny had apparently given him some really good ideas for his sales, and he was thrilled to tell her all about the 3,500-year-old process and the four buyers. Christina listened to his description of the Wise Buyer and envisioned times in her life she'd encountered those kinds. She and Ryan talked for more than an hour about the new ideas he was getting, and was excited to hear that he'd be getting instruction about the rest of the buyers over the remainder of the week.

After a workday that just crawled by, Christina came home and heard about the Cynical Buyer.

"So Bob was in full Cynical Buyer mode at my review," she exclaimed. "No wonder he wouldn't listen to what I was saying—I was totally being defensive, and Cynical Buyers can't stand that! I'm going to need some really good behind-the-scenes information in order to make him happy."

"Yep, maybe you can find some industry facts he doesn't know or something," Ryan suggested.

"I'm sure he knows most of what I could find; he really reads the industry magazines. But maybe I'll call Spencer, see what I can find." Spencer was Cassidy's comptroller, and he and Christina had been friends for years.

"Great idea!" Ryan enthused.

On Wednesday, Christina talked to Spencer and came up with a theory she asked him to test. She believed that different clients needed different things from Cassidy, and she wanted to know whether it would be possible to determine the profit generated on each kind of client. Sure enough, she found the data she needed, and Spencer agreed to keep her conclusions to himself for the time being.

Christina spent Thursday working on more data for what she started thinking of as "Cynical Buyer Bob." That night Ryan told her about the Disinterested Buyer and about integration, and Christina abruptly realized that her meeting might be more complicated than just dealing with "Cynical Bob."

"Ryan, how can I possibly come up with all the stuff Bob's going to throw at me? What if he changes into another kind of buyer?"

"We could try role-playing the meeting, if you wanted."

"That sounds like a really good idea. Let's do it tomorrow night, the boys will be out on a double-date with the Trask sisters."

Friday night was role-playing night for the Millers. Ryan and Christina worked until after curfew (the boys were never on time for curfew on Friday nights, and they'd made it a tradition to stay up late waiting for them). They took turns switching sides, each alternating playing Bob and Christina, until she felt she had a good handle on dealing with the four different buyers Bob could become. They did minimal role-playing for a Disinterested Bob—it was unlikely he'd become disinterested, and they decided if he did, she could always show some skin and tell him to get back into the discussion. But she had solid plans for the rest of the types, and she couldn't wait for her meeting.

Monday morning, Christina marched into Bob's office full of confidence but trying to act humble so as not to appear to be trying to sell herself. Bob opened the conversation.

"So, I'm confused," Bob said, playing with the linked paperclips on his desk. "What is there to talk about? I thought I made myself pretty clear."

"You did, Bob, and that's what I want to talk to you about. As you said, Cassidy is going through some tough times. Margins are down and costs are steady, which means profits are way down."

"Right, at least you were listening."

"I was indeed. So my question: Wouldn't it be great if margins were going up instead of down, and if our costs were going down instead of being steady?"

"Well, of course, duh. So what's the . . ."

"Right," Christina interrupted. "So I've been doing some research over the past week. I have some statistics about what's happening with Cassidy that I'm not sure you're aware of."

Bob's gaze sharpened. "Oh?"

"Yes, I spent some time last week going over the customer surveys we do every year and comparing them to our sales records. What I found was fascinating." Christina took two charts out of her briefcase and put them on Bob's desk for him to read. "The graph on your left shows the margin we're making on people who said in the survey that they chose us on price. As you can see, margins have gone down every year for the past five years for this group."

"Sure, I knew that," Bob said impatiently. "How's that help?"

Christina continued, ignoring Bob's outburst. "The graph on your right shows the margin we're making on people who said in the survey that they chose us because we educate them on the different kinds of insurance. You see there? The margins have been stable or increasing every year."

Bob looked confused. "So you're saying that if we spend more time educating people, we get better margins on them. But we can't do that all the time—it's much more expensive to educate our customers than it is to just get the low-price shoppers."

"True. But we only have to educate them once." Christina pulled out another two charts and placed them on top of the previous ones. "The customers we educate remain our customers for an average of seven years," she said, pointing at the graph on Bob's right. "Whereas the customers who come to us because we have the lowest price stay with us for an average of 1.4 years. We're spending substantially more attracting new customers at a low price point, but then those customers leave us as soon as they find a cheaper offer. The customers we educated stick with us because we are able to give them something they find more valuable than just the lowest price—we give them an education, and they apparently love that.

"My initial numbers indicate we can make twice the profit with half the clients, and we can get our staff back down to forty or fifty hours a week, rather than the sixty to eighty we've all been working since the layoffs."

Bob was clearly impressed. He took all the graphs and sat back in his chair. Christina could tell this meeting was different—he was warming to her. But he wasn't sold yet.

"This is very interesting, Christina. You got this from Spencer?"

Christina guessed Bob had transformed into a Wise Buyer who needed to be told a truth. "Yes, I proposed a theory and he helped me determine whether the theory was accurate. He did the graphics; I just had the ideas."

"Fascinating. And what kind of time does it take for us to educate a consumer, versus the time to sell someone on our low price?"

"I don't know, Bob. But if you can help me with some of the data collection, I think we can come up with the answer to that question within a couple of days, if you want."

"Yes, that'd be good. But how does this all relate to your request to become a marketing rep?"

This was what Christina had been waiting for—an opportunity to redo their previous meeting, when she'd said what she wanted but hadn't been prepared to tell him why he should give it to her.

"I've been doing marketing for the past three years for the Livingston Symphony Orchestra," she started. She reached into her briefcase and pulled out a fact sheet on the benefits the LSO had found in having her work with them. "As you can see, I increased both sales and market recognition in less than six months. I also revamped their web site and marketing materials. Would you believe their web site and their collateral disagreed with each other? The web site focused on educating Livingston's children, whereas some of their brochures focused on how cheap it was to go see the LSO compared with other entertainment options. And others focused how they implemented some really esoteric musical concepts that were of interest to only a very small audience. I helped them come up with a single marketing message and then propagated it through their collateral, web site, and even their answering machine."

"That's interesting. Didn't they have their own marketing staff?"

"No, just a sales team and some volunteers. Some of them put up their web site, others did the collateral, and there were two grandmothers, twins, who put up signs around the neighborhood. It was really haphazard. They needed help, and knew it, so my offer to give them free help was accepted very quickly, even though I didn't have experience at the time.

"I should note that our own marketing is in some-what the same boat. You've brought on several marketing people over the past three years, and each has put their mark on our collateral and web site, but none has changed everything so that it's consistent. And right now we have no marketing person at all, what with the layoffs."

Bob sighed. "True. I had to eliminate all the positions that weren't directly related to bringing in cash. Marketing was obviously part of that."

"That's true, when marketing isn't making the lives of the salespeople easier. That's the role of marketing—to pave the way for speedy and easy sales."

Bob and Christina continued talking for more than an hour. At the end of their meeting, he took her graphs and figures and told her he'd think about it and let her know by the end of the day.

Later, when Christina finally went home she was practically floating. "Ryan! It all worked!" she yelled when she saw him.

He caught her in a big hug. "You got it? Congratulations! That's fantastic, honey! This calls for a celebration, I've made reservations for tonight at Marakesh Restaurant in Parsippany."

"Is that the one with the belly dancer? I've heard about that place!"

"Yep, and I stopped at the liquor store and picked up some great wine."

"You're the best! Let me go change. Are the boys ready?"

"Sure are, although I'll have to tear them away from their cell phones for the night. And apparently Chris has a party he has to attend, so he'll be taking a separate car. But Bobby is with us all evening!"

Christina laughed. Then she paused. Then she roared. Ryan roared back, and they smiled at each other.

Using ROAR for Personal Benefits

Although the value proposition, ROAR process, and four buyers classifications were established for business-to-business (B2B) and business-to-consumer (B2C) purposes, there are principles we've seen in Ryan's story and Christina's personal experience that can benefit your personal, family, or professional life.

In any environment you're always trying to communicate your value and, in many cases, your ideas. The purpose of the value proposition is to make you stand out in a meaningful way so that people can benefit from your presence and existence.

To come up with your personal V.P., first figure out what the other party needs from you. If you're an employee, the need will relate to the job you're doing and to what needs to be done to further your company's goals. In a family situation or family matter, it may be that you're working on communicating ideas for the benefit of the family. In any case, you need to be able to clearly understand the ideas before you come up with your V.P., and to do that, you need to identify who you're communicating it to from the buyer's standpoint.

The Pain

Remember that your goal is not to cause pain for your coworkers, family members, or friends (although some of you may do that without trying). So make sure they know that you understand their pain. That's empathy!

How do you understand their pain? They'll tell you all about it. Listen to them and observe what is happening in their world. This kind of active listening takes practice. You need to quiet your internal voice and listen to them. Do not try to solve their problems; just listen to them and draw out the full story.

Once you've identified the person you're trying to "help," you need to engage them in conversation. This doesn't mean e-mail! You can't get body language and vocal intonation cues when you don't connect audibly and visually. You're missing at least two levels of conversation, and that's not something you can get back. If you can, engage them one-on-one in person.

Do not go in with the goal not of solving the problem; go just for the purposes of inquiry. This will benefit you in two ways. First, you will get answers to questions you ask only if you ask them, not if you do all the answering. And second, you will disarm the person because you're not trying to sell him or her anything (yet).

Here are four lines of questioning that will serve you well in discovering pain.

1. Is there a particular issue at hand? What's happening in the company or the environment? Where are we going from here?
2. Are things going the way you want them to? What's not working?
3. Currently, how are you or how am I affecting any of those things?
4. What would be the perfect world for you?

Once you get your answers, interview and confirm with other people involved (such as coworkers) and determine whether the information you have is the truth.

When you believe you have a handle on the pain (and ideally the pain is not your presence), now it's time to work to generate a simple, objective solution. In most cases it will be obvious. Make sure it's high-level enough. Don't get too granular right now, because you can always do that later. What you want is a straightforward statement that, if it were true, would make people happy.

Now you can begin the discussion and say, "I'm thinking this is the problem." Then follow up with the solution. "Wouldn't it be great if . . ." is an easy way to start the solution sentence. If you get a positive response, you're on the right track.

Now establish why you are the best person to implement the solution. This will be your differentiating factor. This will prove your value in other's eyes.

Christina, for instance, learned that her company was in a race to the bottom in pricing, and she presented a solution to her boss that involved creating a branch devoted to a specialized area. Thinking of her company as a real boutique insurance company will give them cache in other areas, allowing them to come in at a higher profit. She was able to establish herself as someone who is capable of doing this by highlighting the work she did for the Livingston Symphony Orchestra.

Exercise

Take the next two minutes and write down 10 things about yourself that you can bring to the table.

Practice communicating these benefits to a friend or family member who pretends to be the Wise, Cynical or Simple Buyer.

For the Disinterested Buyer, find a fun way to get the person's attention. You might try bringing them a hot fudge sundae or just a balloon.

Ultimately, whenever you are trying to communicate an idea to someone personally, that person will respond as one of the four buyers and the ROAR principles will help you achieve your goals.

Just remember to be secure in your V.P. and be open to the buyer's needs.

Good luck,

Kevin and Dan

Bonus Coupon

Congratulations! By helping us on our quest for the Jewish Superbowl Ring, you have qualified for a free "Using ROAR for Personal Success" webinar with Kevin Daum. Simply go to: www.awesomeroar.com/psshlomoroar and sign up! You'll need the code "jsbrnyt2010." This offer expires March 7, 2011, so sign up today!